Aris & Phillips Hispanic Classics

LUIS VÉLEZ DE GUEVARA

The Mountain Girl from La Vera

La Serrana de la Vera

Translated with a Critical Introduction by

Harley Erdman

LIVERPOOL UNIVERSITY PRESS

First published 2019 by
Liverpool University Press
4 Cambridge Street
Liverpool
L69 7ZU

www.liverpooluniversitypress.co.uk

Copyright © 2019 Harley Erdman

The right of H. Erdman to be identified as the author of this book has been asserted by him in accordance with the Copyright, Designs and Patents Act 1988.

All rights reserved. No part of this book may be reproduced, stored in a retrieval system, or transmitted, in any form or by any means, electronic, mechanical, photocopying, recording, or otherwise, without the prior written permission of the publisher.

British Library Cataloguing-in-Publication data
A British Library CIP record is available

ISBN 978-1-78694-191-6 hardback
ISBN 978-1-78694-192-3 paperback

Typeset by Tara Evans

Cover image: Monument to *La serrana de la Vera*. Garganta la Olla, Spain.
Photo credit: Sarita Hudson

CONTENTS

Acknowledgments v

Introduction 1
The Playwright and His World 2
Sources and Contexts 5
Historical Events 11
Analysis 14
Textual and Stage History 25
A Note on the Translation 28

Bibliography 31

La Serrana de la Vera / The Mountain Girl from La Vera 35

Notes 248

ACKNOWLEDGMENTS

I owe a debt of gratitude to C. George Peale. More than anyone else, he has opened up the eyes of our field to Luis Vélez de Guevara and to this play. Most especially, his generosity in providing his and William R. Manson's Spanish edition has sped and facilitated my work.

I also want to thank Harrison Meadows, whose perceptive paper at the 2016 ASTR working session arguing for a trans lens on Gila sparked my interest in this play.

My colleague and collaborator Gina Kaufmann and I are in the process of adapting the play for the stage. It's been a joy talking about the play with Gina, sharing my materials, and batting around ideas. Her insights into the theatrical dimensions of the work have been invaluable.

Finn Lefevre read a draft of the translation and gave thoughtful responses. I owe them a big thanks for their insights into the play's dramaturgy and what it means to view Gila as trans.

My students in Theater 321 in the fall of 2017 were the first to read the translation aloud. Their enthusiasm for the play has helped to keep me forging ahead.

I have had a wonderful experience working with Liverpool University Press. I want to thank Chloe Johnson for her helpfulness and professionalism. It is a great pleasure to be working again with Jonathan Thacker. I am indebted to his encouragement and expertise.

Finally, I am grateful to Sarita, Jonah, and Cara – my family. Their love and support make everything possible. I am lucky.

INTRODUCTION

This bilingual edition presents Luis Vélez de Guevara's 1613 play *La Serrana de la Vera* (*The Mountain Girl from La Vera*) for the first time ever in English.[1] This long-forgotten tragedy has come back into focus in recent years because of its extraordinary protagonist, Gila, a peasant girl who calls herself a man and takes pride in doing things men do and doing them one better. She hunts, fences, gambles, ploughs, even bull-fights. In feats of strength and prowess, she outshines the men around her, and relishes bragging about it. Gila also tries to catch the attention of Queen Isabel, with whom she is in love. Gila's downfall comes when she is seduced and betrayed by a high-ranking military officer, Captain Don Lucas de Carvajal, who promises her power and status but abandons her in order to get revenge for his own earlier public humiliation at her hands. Desperate and outraged, Gila takes to the mountains, where she lives the life of an outlaw, murdering virtually every man she comes across, including, eventually, Don Lucas. In the end, Gila is brought to justice and publically executed in grisly fashion with the consent of Ferdinand and Isabella, the same monarchs she admires.

As many critics have commented, *Mountain Girl* is a strange, unsettling play, 'una obra muy problemática' ('a very problematic work').[2] It features broad comedy, even slapstick, but in the end veers into violence and tragedy. It has many realistic touches, but also is replete with exaggerated and grotesque elements characteristic of folk tales, legend, and myth. It lays out plausible motivations for its characters' actions yet has these characters undergo unexpected, seemingly unexplained shifts in behavior. Its historical backdrop (the play is set in the late 1400s) features famous characters from Spanish history, but the relationship of this subplot to the main action of the play is puzzling. Finally, *Mountain Girl* features many tropes and character types common to early modern Spanish theater but handles these elements in ways different from other plays of its time.

---

1 I follow C. George Peale's practice of capitalizing *Serrana* in the Spanish title, suggesting that the play references the specific *Serrana* of legend rather than a generic *serrana*, while also distinguishing Vélez de Guevara's play from Lope de Vega's *La serrana de la Vera*. Most critical literature on the play follows standard Spanish orthographic convention, rendering it *La serrana de la Vera*.

2 Parr and Albuixech 17.

For all these reasons, it is fair to call the play 'non-normative,' befitting a title character who is non-normative. Gila has been variously labeled by critics over the past generation as manly, irregular, monstrous, feminist, homosexual, bisexual, ambiguous, lesbian, transsexual, hybrid, and queer. It may be that the contemporary category 'transgender' offers the best frame for Gila – that is, someone at odds with the gender assigned to them at birth or whose combination of masculine and feminine facets means that they, to cite Christopher Shelley's criteria in *Transpeople*, 'would prefer to be able to retain ambivalence, either in body or comportment' (8).[3] To put it another way: Gila is gender-queer. Moreover, Vélez has constructed his play so as to make audiences sympathize with this character who so strikingly upsets the gender binary.

Mountain Girl has a lot else to offer. It is a great piece of theater, full of dramatic confrontations, colorful vignettes, striking moments of music and spectacle, and comic relief. The fact that Vélez wrote the play for a specific actress – the acclaimed Jusepa Vaca – adds to our understanding of the play in the dimension of performance. Finally, the surviving autograph manuscript of the play is marked up – whether by the playwright or someone from Vaca's theater company – so as to give a highly specific indication of what sections of the play might have been edited, cut, or censured for performance, thus offering a singular window into the distinction between what playwrights wrote and what ultimately ended up on stage. All in all, *Mountain Girl* deserves wide attention as a piece of dramatic literature, a cultural document, and a performance script.

The Playwright and His World

Luis Vélez de Guevara (1579–1644) is gaining recognition as one of the leading playwrights of early modern Spain. This 'Golden Age,' which in Spain has been traditionally labeled the *Siglo de Oro* (Golden Century), corresponds to the roughly hundred-year period from 1580 to 1680 that saw an outpouring of cultural production, ranging from the paintings of Diego de Velázquez to the fiction of Miguel de Cervantes to the imaginative

3 I am indebted to Harrison Meadows, whose paper at the 2016 ASTR Working Session first articulated the idea of Gila as 'transgender' to me. Of the writers who address Gila's gender non-normativity, Matthew Stroud's queer reading of her in *Plot Twists and Critical Turns* has had a major impact on the field. Bergmann, Boyle, Lundelius, Martín (2008), Strother, Otero-Torres (1997, 1998), and Tropé have also published excellent scholarship that has influenced my thinking about Gila and the play.

literary works of writers such as Francisco de Quevedo and Luis de Góngora. Thousands of plays were produced during this time for performances in public theaters known as *corrales*: open-air courtyards that accommodated up to 2000 people for daily billings that featured full-length plays known as *comedias* interlaced with songs, dances, and comic sketches. Unlike the public theaters in England, the *corrales* featured women in the roles of female characters. Indeed, actresses were among the most celebrated performers. All the major playwrights fashioned commanding opportunities for these women, resulting in a repertory that is a treasure trove of female roles.

Vélez was born at precisely the historical moment that many *corrales* were being created across Spain. The prime years of his adulthood – the first few decades of the seventeenth century – coincide with the flourishing of *comedias* that adhered to the dramaturgical model put forth by Lope de Vega (1562–1635), the era's most popular and influential playwright. These *comedias* invariably had three acts, mixed comic and serious elements, and were written in rhymed verse for theater companies that featured, if not exactly stock characters, at least company members who specialized in certain types of roles, including the *dama* (leading lady), *galán* (leading man), and *gracioso* (clown or comic sidekick).

Vélez was a prolific playwright. He probably wrote over 400 plays, of which 70 *comedias* and 20 short plays are extant. Frequently cast as a 'follower' of Lope, he has been relegated to secondary or tertiary status, a minor playwright even relative to other contemporaries (for example, Tirso de Molina) who also followed Lope's model of freewheeling, accessible, action-packed plays. The reputation has stuck to him of being a malcontent, complainer, grumbler, rebel, *pedigüeño* (someone always asking for money), though recent scholarship has called some of these assumptions into question.[4] He was virtually forgotten in the 19th century, the age of romanticism, which prized the genius of originality. Vélez, in contrast, almost always adapted histories and legends rather than generating original plots.[5] Only in the early 20th century did his work slowly come back into light. That effort has been reinvigorated in the 21st century by the tireless efforts of C. George Peale, who, building on work by William R. Manson, has released scholarly editions of many of his plays.

---

4 See Bolaños (2001) 9, and Urzáiz 22, for biographical information on Vélez, recently challenged by Martín Ojeda and Peale, who meticulously uncover the roots of these assumptions and myths in these brief biographies.

5 Profeti 3.

Enough is known about the playwright's life to give us a rough outline. Luis Vélez de Santander was born in 1579 in Écija, near Seville, to petty middle-class circumstances. His father was a lawyer; his mother, the daughter of one. He received a Bachelor of Arts degree from the nearby University of Osuna in 1596. Except for a brief period in the early 1600s when he served as a soldier in Italy, he spent virtually the entirety of his adult life in formal service to a series of powerful patrons – first, to Cardinal Rodrigo de Castro, then to the Count of Saldaña, and then to the Duke of Osuna, before becoming 'usher to the chamber' of the Prince of Wales during his visit to Spain to arrange a marriage with the Infanta María Ana in 1623. (The marriage never materialized.) Vélez then briefly became *mayordomo* (chief steward) to Carlos, Arch Duke of Austria, in 1624.[6] Finally, in 1625, he secured the appointment that he would hold for the rest of his life: 'usher to the chamber' of King Felipe IV. This position, of a partly ceremonial nature, provided him a place of prestige in the court of Madrid, though apparently not enough income to support a family. His playwriting both prior to and during this appointment was therefore probably a way to supplement this modest living.

Vélez was married four times. In two of the first three marriages, he was left a widower due to spouses who died young – in one case, in childbirth. His fourth and final marriage, to María López de Palacios in 1625, lasted the rest of his life. He had at least seven children, including three sons with his second wife, Úrsula Ramisi y Bravo (to whom he was married at the time of *Mountain Girl*), and four daughters with María López. One son from the former marriage, Juan, went on to become a dramatist as well. A tender and unusual touch to the *Mountain Girl* manuscript is Vélez's inscription of dedication to Úrsula and their three sons. It appears at the beginning of all three acts.

Overall, the picture is of a multi-talented literary man with a flair for bold, colorful plays, often about kings and leaders, as well as a penchant for comedy, satire, and social commentary. According to one contemporary account, he was an '*hombre chistoso*' (funny man or joker).[7] It is instructive that he was asked to oversee a comic writing festival in 1637. His talents and energies seemed to have outstripped the positions he was able to attain for himself as a person of modest background.

Though from a family of respectable, practicing Christians, Vélez

6 Austria in these high aristocratic titles references the Spanish crown's Hapsburg family lineage, not the geographical location of the kingdom.

7 See Bolaños (2001), 20.

potentially suffered the stigma of being 'New Christian' – that is, of Jewish ancestry.[8] The considerable swath of Iberia controlled by Christian rulers in the Middle Ages had large Jewish and Muslim populations; in some communities, they outnumbered Christians. Starting in the 1400s, a series of edicts and decrees, brutally enforced by the newly created Inquisition, effectively eliminated any openly practicing non-Christians from these territories. Meanwhile, in 1492, the last remaining Moorish-Islamic kingdom in Iberia fell under Christian control. The result was that, by the turn of the 16th century, all of Spain was by law monolithically Christian. In this lengthy and violent cultural upheaval, the critical year of which was 1492, many Jewish families ended up leaving Spain. Many, however, converted to Christianity and came to be known as *conversos* (converts) or 'New Christians,' to distinguish them from 'Old Christians' who reputedly could trace their bloodlines to places in Iberia untainted by Moorish or Jewish settlement. Ironically, many New Christians went on to enjoy positions of power and prestige in 16th- and 17th-century Spain, but only because they were able to shed, hide, or repudiate their family origins.[9] Vélez's shedding of his original name surname 'Santander' and taking on the more reputable Christian name 'Guevara' has been seen as such a move.[10] What is distinctive about Vélez is not that he was a writer of *converso* origin but that his own sly winking reference to his heritage in his novel *El diablo cojuelo* helps us to establish him as one. He was one of the few literary figures of Spain's Golden Age willing to admit it.[11]

Sources and Contexts

'Manly Women' and Serranas

Spanish Golden Age playwrights frequently turned to source material to generate ideas for their plays. Such sources included novellas, folk tales, ballads, legends, histories, and lives of saints. Sometimes a single stanza of an old ballad would be enough to inspire an entire play. Successful plays

8 Martín Ojeda and Peale have recently looked into this ancestry, which, in terms of practicing Jews in the playwright's family, dates back to before 1492. Their argument, which challenges long-received notions about Vélez, would make any such stigma faint and remote.

9 See Lee for an excellent analysis of what it meant to be a *converso* at this time.

10 See Urzáiz 39. Again, this has been challenged recently by Martín Ojeda and Peale.

11 For the above short biography, I have drawn on Bolaños (2001), Davies, Urzáiz, and Ziomek and Hughes. Davies is particularly specific in dealing with the references to *converso* heritage in Vélez's writing.

then spurred imitations, which in turn inspired new versions of these plays, creating a dense intertextual web of dramatic works.

In the broadest terms, Gila exemplifies the Golden Age trope of the *mujer varonil* or 'manly woman,' a tremendously popular figure in plays of the time, and one that seemed to have particular appeal to Vélez: one-quarter of his surviving plays feature some version of this character.[12] The *mujer varonil* always enacts some sort of gender transgression, either by displaying masculine characteristics, dressing as a man, or creating some gender-related subterfuge to achieve her ends. Audiences at the time were drawn to these vibrant, sympathetic heroines, and seemed to have delighted in seeing them cross social boundaries that would have been proscribed to women off stage.[13] For many male viewers (and some women), there was also the eroticism of seeing women dressed as men on stage, a costuming that would have been more revealing than standard female attire of the time. Interestingly, reverse transgressions – the dandy or effeminate man – were much less common on stage, and very rarely did male characters dress as women. Given femininity's traditional subordination to masculinity in the hierarchy of power and status, it makes sense that a woman who acted masculine could be applauded as a heroine and protagonist, while a man who acted feminine was a figure of shame and scorn.[14]

Critics have articulated many varieties of the *mujer varonil,* some of which find resonance in *Mountain Girl.* These include the *bella cazadora* (beautiful huntress), who echoes Artemis/Diana of classical mythology; the *bandolera*, (highwaywoman), who assaults passersby on rural backroads; the *donzella guerrera* (warrior maiden); and the *asesina*, (murderess). All of these types were in particular vogue in the early decades of the 17th century.[15]

The particular incarnation of *mujer varonil* that is the foundation for Vélez's play is the *serrana*, a term which generically could refer to any young rural woman of Spain's highlands but more specifically invoked the trope of a dangerous female of the mountains. The prototype is found in Juan Ruiz's 14th-century epic poem, *El libro de buen Amor* (*The Book of Good Love*), which depicts an enticing mountain woman who lives among high

12 Lundelius 220.

13 McKendrick has written the most influential book on the *mujer varonil*, though her conclusions have been disputed by many, including Bradbury.

14 See, for example, Martín (2008), 114.

15 Parr and Albuixech elaborate on how *Mountain Girl* merges many of these tropes. For a description of the warrior maiden tradition, see Martín (2008), 116–23.

passes associated with beasts and bandits and takes the sexual initiative with male travelers she encounters. This *serrana* tradition, as Adrienne Laskier Martín has shown in her *Erotic Philology of Golden Age Spain*, casts the mountainous regions of Spain as dark zones of transgression – deformed and sinful places, 'inhospitable wastelands inhabited by monstrous and violent women who beat and rape male travelers.' Here, a mountain range becomes the supine 'female erotic body par excellence' (155).

Related to this larger Iberian tradition are legends associated with La Vera, a highland region in west central Spain, in the northern part of Extremadura, not far from Portugal. A number of traditional ballads recorded in 15th-century *romanceros* (ballad books) tell the story of a *serrana*, originally from the small town of Garganta la Olla.[16] These ballads were part of a larger oral tradition which would have been known to Vélez's audiences in 1613 and which have continued to be part of popular lore. Somewhat less monstrous than other *serranas,* Garganta la Olla's mountain girl is a fair-skinned beauty who invites men up to her mountain hut for a meal and a sexual encounter, then murders them so they will not go back to town to spread word of her dishonor. Martín has likened her to a black widow spider who kills men after mating (159). The ballads are always told from the point of view of an unnamed male narrator who has managed to survive the encounter. In one version:

Allá en Garganta la Olla,
en la Vera de Plasencia,
salteóme una serrana,
blanca, rubia, ojimorena.
Trae el cabello trenzado
debajo de una montera
y, porque no la estorbara,
muy corta la faldamenta.
Entre los montes andaba
de una en otra ribera,
con una honda en sus manos
y en sus hombros una flecha.
Tomárame por la mano

16 There are around 20 different versions of the ballad, according to the celebrated ethnographers the Pidal brothers, as cited in Parr and Albuixech (19). McKendrick gives it as 21 versions (277). Strother argues that the play is not sourced in the ballad tradition per se but in a larger 'mythic system' that predates and transcends any specific version of it (166).

y me llevara a su cueva;
por el camino que iba
tantas de las cruces viera.
Atrevíme y preguntéle
qué cruces eran aquellas,
y me respondió diciendo
que de hombres que muerto hubiera.
Esto me responde y dice,
como entre medio risueña:
Y así haré de ti, cuitado,
cuando mi voluntad sea.
Diome yesca y pedernal
para que lumbre encendiera,
y mientras que la encendía,
aliña una grande cena;
de perdices y conejos
su pretina saca llena,
y después de haber cenado
me dice: –Cierra la puerta.
Hago como que la cierro,
y la dejé entreabierta.
Desnudóse y desnudéme
y me hace acostar con ella.
Cansada de sus deleites
muy bien dormida se queda,
y en sintiéndola dormida
sálgome la puerta afuera.
Los zapatos en la mano
llevo porque no me sienta,
y poco a poco me salgo
y camino a la ligera.
Más de una legua había andado
sin revolver la cabeza,
y cuando mal me pensé
yo la cabeza volviera.
Y en esto la vi venir,
bramando como una fiera,
saltando de canto en canto,

brincando de peña en peña.
Aguarda [me dice], aguarda,
espera, mancebo, espera,
me llevarás una carta
escrita para mi tierra.
Toma, llévala a mi padre,
dirásle que quedo buena.
Enviadla vos con otro,
o sed vos la mensajera.[17]

(There in Garganta la Olla
In La Vera of Plasencia,
I was assaulted by a serrana,
Of fair skin, light hair, and dark eyes.
Under her head-covering
She wore her hair in braids,
And so as to be unencumbered,
She had a very short skirt.
She wandered in the mountains
From one river valley to another,
With a slingshot in her hands
And an arrow over her shoulder.
She took me by the hand
And led me to her cave,
And along the way there,
I could see many crosses.
I dared to ask her
What the crosses were for,
And she answered, telling me
That they were men she'd killed.
So she answered, and then
She says, half-laughing:
Beware, I'll do the same to you
If the feeling strikes me.
She gave me flint and tinder
For me to light a fire,

17 I am using the version of the ballad reprinted in McKendrick (277), taken from a Menéndez y Pelayo appendix to an anthology of lyric poetry. For other versions, see Gutiérrez Macías.

And while I lit it,
She arranged a large supper,
Her waist bag stuffed full
Of partridges and rabbits,
And after we had suppered,
She tells me: Close the door.
I pretend to close it,
But left it half open.
She got undressed, and so did I,
And she had me go to bed with her.
Exhausted from her delights,
She fell asleep very soundly,
And when I sensed she was sleeping,
I slipped out the door.
My shoes, I kept in my hand,
So she wouldn't hear me.
And little by little I made my way out,
Treading very carefully.
I had walked more than a league
Before I turned my head,
And then I made the mistake
Of turning my head around:
In that moment, I saw her coming,
Roaring like a beast,
Jumping from stone to stone,
Leaping from cliff to cliff.
Stop, [she tells me], stop,
Wait, young man, wait,
You will carry a letter from me,
Written for the land I'm from.
Take it, bring it to my father,
Tell him I am all right.
You can send it with another
Or you can be the messenger.)

Lope de Vega also wrote a play entitled *La serrana de la Vera* (c. 1599–1600). This work draws on the same ballad tradition and was a likely point of reference for Vélez. Lope's version, however, has only faint similarities to Vélez's. The one direct point of coincidence is a female character who takes to the hills partway through the play to become a *bandolera* to avenge an insult done to her by a man. Lope's *serrana*, Leonarda, however, serves as protagonist for what ultimately plays out as romantic comedy: the tale of a noble woman who through a series of mix-ups and misunderstandings temporarily takes refuge in the mountains. The play ends with her happy marriage and reintegration into society. Vélez, in contrast, allies himself more closely to the dangerous, forbidding *serrana* of the ballad tradition. In working from the ballad material, Vélez crafted the bolder, more violent and disturbing play, one that pushed limits and challenged conventions.

Vélez de Guevara's version seems to have found an audience in its time too, for it in turn inspired other dramatic versions of the *serrana* legend, including one performed by Jusepa Vaca herself in 1618 for Corpus Christi celebrations.[18]

Historical Events

Though not exactly a history play, *Mountain Girl* has a defined historical milieu. It features, in supporting roles, illustrious personages from Spanish history. Vélez situates us in the reign of the famed *Reyes Católicos* (the Catholic Kings), Ferdinand and Isabella. Their marriage in 1469 joined their respective kingdoms of Aragon and Castile into a powerful alliance that, after surviving a bloody Iberian civil war against Portugal and its allies, led to the unification of the modern nation now known as Spain and ushered in, with due brutality, a great age of Spanish imperial power. The momentous year in Ferdinand and Isabel's reign was 1492, when they conquered the kingdom of Granada (the last Islamic territory in Spain), expelled all practicing Jews, and authorized Columbus's long-sought journey to explore a western trade route to the Indies. For early 17th-century audiences, these monarchs were heroic figures – the founding father and mother of the nation – and it was not unusual for them to be featured in plays, most famously Lope's *Fuente Ovejuna*, written around the same time as *Mountain Girl*. Though it is common to think of Ferdinand and Isabella as Spain's first modern monarchs, they also can be seen as the last medieval rulers of Spain in that they wielded power personally; with no fixed capital, they travelled constantly throughout their territories to administer disputes, dispense justice, and resolve grievances (Kamen 27). This highly mobile, personalized aspect of their rule is accurately represented in *Mountain Girl*.

18 See Reyes Peña 86, as well as Boyle 79, for more on this performance.

Mountain Girl telescopes, with considerable creative license, various events from the late 1400s. In Act One, we hear news of the siege of Alhama, a key moment in Ferdinand and Isabella's decades-long, on-again-off-again war for Granada. Ostensibly, then, we are in 1482, the year of that siege.[19] However the play also dwells at length on the death of their only son, eighteen-year-old Juan, Prince of Asturias. The news of his grave condition, recounted at the end of Act One, was actually delivered in 1497. The play presents the circumstances of his death as quasi-heroic, involving a daring ride on horseback. In real life, they were murkier, and may have involved either tuberculosis or, as was rumored, sexual over-exertion. Vélez is thus giving his own highly subjective version of historical events, using them flexibly and strategically for thematic and dramatic counterpoint, while also placing his narrative in an era roughly contemporaneous with the *serrana* of popular ballads. This is in sharp contrast to Lope, who weaves no history into his *La serrana de la Vera*; the circumstances are presented there as contemporary to the time of his audience. It should be recalled, the *serrana* ballads likewise have no historical or public dimension. Vélez deploys history, therefore, to give his play a social-political dimension, to invest it with proportions of myth and legend associated with great events and people of the past.

Rodrigo Téllez de Girón is also a well-known personage from Spanish history. In his powerful inherited position as Master of Calatrava, he leads a military order that was pivotal to the Christian Reconquest of Spain. He also figures prominently in *Fuente Ovejuna*. Gila's antagonist, Captain Don Lucas de Carvajal, is, as far as I can tell, a fictional creation, but the Carvajals were indeed a powerful clan from Plasencia who were closely allied with Ferdinand and Isabella; by the late 1400s, the Carvajals were already occupying important religious and administrative posts in Castile.[20] The name would have been an illustrious one to audiences in 1613, although, as I will show, not one without associations of tainted lineage.

Mountain Girl depicts a period before the modern nation-state, and therefore a society in which there were no standing armies. Ferdinand and

19 More subtle anachronism is built into this timeline, since Ferdinand and Isabella did not themselves gain direct control of Plasencia from local nobles until 1485 (Kamen 21). The play presents them as already having control over Plasencia, though various moments – including Giraldo's resistance to the Captain in the opening scene – suggest their rule there is not yet fully implemented.

20 'Carvajal' is sometimes given as 'Caravajal.' I have standardized the orthography for this edition.

Isabella were dependent on militias of Christian warriors like the Order of Calatrava – founded in the Middle Ages for the purposes of the Crusades – for military endeavors. They were also dependent on alliances with local noblemen like the fictional Don Lucas, who could muster local troops for national service, as Don Lucas attempts to do in Garganta la Olla, one of the towns under his sway. In Act Three, Gila is hunted down by the *Hermandad* (Brotherhood), which here is portrayed as a sort of royally authorized posse. These were in fact local police forces in Castile that, after the 1460s, came under the control of Ferdinand and Isabella (Kamen 17–19). Though off on the details, *Mountain Girl* does nevertheless portray with rough accuracy the array of armed forces that by the 1480s were working together under the banner of Ferdinand and Isabella to impose order upon and extirpate dissent within Spain.[21]

This heroic historical landscape of Christian nationalist reconquest, of peninsular purification and unification, was a rich source of inspiration for the *comedia*. It was a landscape where manly, warrior women were apt to be found. Tirso de Molina's *Antona García* (published in 1635) is another play about a larger-than-life peasant woman from western Spain who undertakes heroic deeds of courage and strength. Though she is based on an historical figure who fought in the wars against Portugal in the 1470s, Tirso's treatment of her is exaggerated, colorful, folkloric. Less folkloric in treatment is Laurencia in *Fuente Ovejuna* – another fierce daughter of small-town Spain who, in this case, leads an uprising against a brutal overlord. She is a fictional character, though the events themselves are historical to 1476. All these 17th-century versions of 15th-century women bathe in the glow of the savvy and powerful Isabella, the last woman to fully share in the power of the Spanish throne. Isabella presides over a psycho-historical landscape that, from the nostalgic perspective of 1613, engendered women of uncommon fierceness and strength. The historical milieu therefore raises the stakes for Gila's conflict, amplifying and intensifying it, even though her story leads in a far more tragic direction than those of other *mujeres varoniles*. In fact, most striking about Vélez's play is how it takes tropes, ideas, and characters common to the day and inverts, challenges, or complicates them. The result is a play full of surprises.

21 See Kamen for the most thorough analysis of this dynamic.

Analysis

Gila

Most interpretations of *Mountain Girl* hinge on how one decides to read – or stage – Gila. On one hand, as Melveena McKendrick argues, 'That Luis Vélez disapproves of Gila there can be no doubt' (117). Therefore, her execution at the end of the play is fitting punishment for her 'arrogant feminism' (118). Ruth Lundelius similarly sees the ending as a vindication of traditional values, which demand severe punishment for Gila's 'intolerable deviation from the norm' (235). The ending, therefore, is a 'profound moral lesson' (237), even if there are lingering complexities. This perspective is echoed in part by the more recent scholarship of Hélène Tropé, who argues that the end of the play, like all plays of early modern Spain, asserts the power of dominant male values over those who would transgress. She cites José Antonio Maravall, who put forward the influential thesis that Golden Age theater ultimately is reactionary – that is, in service to seventeenth-century power structures in the way it dramatizes acts of punishment (via tragedy) and reintegration (via comedy). In these readings, *Mountain Girl* is a play that not only represents coercion but enacts it, though Tropé, among others, clearly aligns herself with Gila, who suffers at the hands of this brutal system of which the play's dramaturgy is itself a part.

Most readings of the play, however, take issue with the notion that the narrative positions Gila as unreservedly deserving of condemnation. I would argue that there would be little or no contemporary interest in the play if it were not for the fact that *Mountain Girl* is structured to give audiences – both then and now – the desire to see Gila, at least in part, as a sympathetic character, a tragic figure, a heroic rebel, and that her execution at the end somehow encompasses crimes against the social order beyond the ones she actually commits. This strand of criticism, departing from Maravall, argues for complexity and nuance in our reading of the *comedia* in general and this play in particular. Theater is a dialogic form that shows characters in action, in conflict with themselves and with others; plays may be permeated with ideology, but they are highly imperfect vehicles for conveying it, for putting forth theses, for enforcing a social code. This becomes even more true when embodied in performance, where staging and interpretation regularly subvert and undermine what may seem evident in a script. Henry Sullivan has argued that the fundamental element underlying all *comedias* is Lacanian: the 'unresolvable dialectic' between Desire and the Law (333).

The end of *Mountain Girl*, I would argue, does not and cannot provide closure or catharsis.

Mountain Girl has the conventional *comedia* three-act structure, with each act leaning toward the Aristotelian unities of time and place. Act One takes places in Garganta la Olla and nearby Plasencia over the course of one day. Act Two takes place an undefined amount of time later – perhaps a few weeks or a month – in Garganta la Olla and Salamanca, with the action elapsing over the course of a day and night. Act Three takes place many months later (the time elapsed is once again ill-defined) in the sierra of La Vera and Plasencia, as well as Salamanca, over the course of what seems to be two days.[22] A central dramatic spine – Gila's conflict with the Captain – guides the action but does not dominate it. Much of the stage time is spent on a series of loose episodes with recurring characters. Repetition and return amplify the play's impact. In each act Gila has a confrontation with her nemesis, the Captain. In each act, she has an encounter with her friend and would-be lover, the rustic comedian Mingo. In each act, we glimpse Gila's friendship with other women, notably her cousin Madalena. In each, she confronts the misogynistic roughneck, Andrés. Each act features at least one prominent, highly ceremonial appearance of the King and Queen, in which we see them negotiate the devastating circumstances of their son's demise. Each act ends with some interruption or disruption of Gila's fortune. The comedic and the serious not only alternate but intermingle, with the tone shifting moment to moment. On the cusp of killing Mingo, for example, Gila engages him incongruously in light-hearted banter about the state of things in their village. The effect is both bizarre and poignant. As episodes recur, the stakes get raised. The largely lighthearted vignettes of Act One (Gila festively at play in Plasencia) give way to ones of more intensity and tenderness in Act Two (Gila fending off or accepting lovers) and then hurtle into extremes of violence and alienation in Act Three, where, in the wilds of the sierra, Gila mostly makes good on her vow to kill every man she meets.

Throughout, the play trades on spectacle and Gila's spectacular body, including her public performance of self. She asserts her identity through public or quasi-public stage-able acts (riding in on horseback, fencing, bullfighting, plowing, etc.) as if her extraordinary nature depends desperately on her ability to demonstrate to audiences that she can successfully do the things that men do. Even her murders are enacted performatively,

22 I take the play's time/place scheme largely from Bolaños (2001).

commemorated visibly with crosses.[23] Little is private to her; her most private act (her liaison with the Captain) is quickly made public by her within moments of her betrayal. Even when she is alone, her identity is performative and spectacular – stagey – such as the opening of Act Two, when we see her wielding a plough. The play makes Gila knowable through deploying her as spectacle, and thus, as Margaret Boyle argues, 'cements the multifaceted interrelationship between violence, spectacle, and exemplarity' in early modern Baroque culture (92). It is no wonder that the play's final reveal is the spectacular tableau of her transfigured body.

Contrasting Vélez's version of the *serrana* legend to other versions highlights his ideological strategy. Lope's *serrana*, like countless other *mujeres varoniles*, merely plays at being a man for particular reasons that, once resolved, lead back to her normalized status as bride in a comedy that ends happily.[24] Gila, in contrast, eschews the conventional complications of comedy; the play resists any sense that Gila is merely playing a role or going through a phase. Gila cannot be reconciled to normative society.

Most instructive is Vélez's complete inversion of the source ballad. The *serrana* ballads are all framed from the point of view of the male traveler who comes upon her in the woods. They allow us to glimpse the *serrana* only in her most wild state: sexualized, violent, cunning. The ballads end triumphantly for the narrator, who tricks and disgraces the *serrana*, using his wits to survive his encounter with this murderer. Moreover, the ballad *serrana* has no back story, motivation, justification, dimensionality. She is a kind of monster: the Other. Vélez works backwards from this core encounter so that by the time we encounter Gila in the condition that most epitomizes her monstrosity, we have been shown a series of circumstances that undermines the ballad's narrative assumptions. We have experienced her as a sympathetic human being with desires, ambitions, and talents. We have seen her standing up for her community, family, and friends. We have seen her fending off misogynists and intruders. We have seen the cruel betrayal and humiliation that leads her to violence. Finally, we see that she is motivated not by sexual desire, let alone ravenous sexual appetite, but by a sincere need to avenge her honor. The play is thus a rejoinder to the ballad, a kind of legal brief on her behalf. Even amid the excess of her killing two thousand men, there is a disconnect between the circumstances of her claims and what we see on

23 See Strother in this context, for the way Gila consciously self-mythologizes.

24 See Parr and Albuixech 22, for example. They offer an excellent overview of Lope's play in relationship to Vélez's.

stage. Of the five male travelers she encounters in Act Three, there is one (Ferdinand) who she sets free, and another (Mingo) about whom she seems indecisive enough that her hesitation results in his making it out alive. Of the three remaining 'prey,' two (Andrés and the Captain) are clearly being repaid for insults incurred against her early in the play. That leaves only the unnamed traveler near the top of Act Three as a man killed without cause, yet his coarseness and cockiness suggest he is of similar character to the other men whose lives she takes. To cite Harrison Meadows:

> The scenes that depict her murderous revenge against all men are relatively brief in relation to the first two acts that are dedicated to Gila's character development, and even the scenes that depict her serial murders mostly focus on the death of Lucas, which can be considered poetic justice. In other words, the economy of the narrative suggests that her murders are not what the play is truly concerned with, nor the genuine trigger for the final scene. (4)

Furthermore, Reina Ruiz points out that Gila's chosen method of murder does not constitute stage violence: relative to other methods, throwing a victim off a cliffs has a sanitized, potentially comic quality that obviates having to deal with an on-stage corpse.[25]

Darci Strother has also argued how Gila is far more sympathetic than the *serrana* of the ballads. She is, for example, conspicuously chaste, killing men *before* she sleeps with them; she gives up her virginity to the Captain only because she has been tricked. She is therefore more of a Diana – a mythic figure, a goddess – than a cruel *serrana*.[26] I would add that even when Gila is arguably at her most monstrous, she shows humanity and tenderness, such as the interlude in Act Three with the little girl, Pascuala. The final tableau of her execution, tied to a stake and pierced by arrows, is explicitly mentioned by Pascuala as looking like St. Sebastian. The play leaves us, then, with a spectacle of Christian martyrdom. As Boyle argues, the ending is too complicated to be merely cautionary; it is meant to leave us 'awestruck' in the way that it positions Gila as a penitential figure, who also accepts responsibility for her actions, as if the subject of an auto-da-fe.[27]

Critics grapple with this complexity, contradiction: murderer as martyr,

---

25 Personal communication to author at AHCT conference, El Paso, April 2018.

26 See Strother, especially 70.

27 A number of commentators have also seen eroticism in this final tableau. Martín (2008) calls it 'morbidly erotic' (66), while Stroud (2007) notes how St. Sebastian has become an erotic icon in gay male culture. I would add that her visual association with a male saint contributes to her status as someone outside gender norms.

human being as monster, woman as man, victim as victimizer, freedom fighter as outlaw. For Matthew Stroud, whose *Plot Twists and Critical Turns* influentially applies queer theory to the *comedia*, Gila's importance resides in the way she 'insists on her own value and significance, thus causing a problem for the men by producing a surfeit of conflicting values: she subordinates her value as an exchange object onto her signification as a human subject participating fully in her society' (128). In this economy, women who assert themselves as subjects, rather than objects, are dangerous. Influenced by queer theorist Eve Sedgwick, Stroud's reading of Gila argues that her actions in the first half of the play pose a system based on heterosociality: equal relationships between women and men. Such a system of relations was unknown in seventeenth-century Spain, where no woman could be friend or rival to a man without being a sexual object. 'When she places herself in the system as a man, she destroys the basic homosocial nature of patriarchal, homosocial society' (134). Thus, for Stroud, her submission to penetration by the Captain turns her into an object and represents the failure of heterosociality. Gila's only remaining recourse is to become the outlaw we see in Act Three: seducing men by promising penetration/domination, and then turning the tables by penetrating/dominating them. Stroud's argument is in line with Dámaris Otero-Torres (1997), who asserts that Gila is radical because she asserts matrimony not as an end in itself but as a stepping stone to power, as it is for men (138).

Along parallel lines, Emilie Bergmann emphasizes the radical nature of Gila's accomplishment: she is the rare woman who avenges her own honor, a point Gila makes repeatedly upon her arrest. Catalyzed into crime by this crisis, she ends up usurping the role of her own father, in whom responsibility lay for undoing such an affront. Thus, there is logic in Gila's choice to surrender not to the state but to her father. At the same time, Bergmann argues, the play re-inscribes Gila as part animal, as she was in some versions of the legend, through the constant visual association of her with beasts, as well as her ultimate animalistic act of biting off her father's ear. Carolina Palacios Diazceballos asserts that Gila today strikes us as a 'mujer independiente, personaje "modern" en quien radica lo que tambien se puede apreciar como la sorpendiente modernidad de la obra.' (237); ('an independent woman, a modern character, in whom is rooted what can be appreciated as the surprising modernity of the work), though her rebelliousness makes her more of a romantic figure, in the nineteenth-century sense, than a classical one. For Tropé, Gila ultimately is a tragic figure, and the end of the play makes us feel ill at ease: her abuse at hands of the Captain is not socially repaired because her tragedy is one of a woman who must take justice into her own hands because men will not or cannot do it for her. It is striking, I would argue, that the spectacle of Gila's death seems to move the women (Madalena, Pascuala, Isabella) to pity far more than the men.

Gila confounds gender norms by repeatedly calling herself a man and by partaking in acts of exaggerated, even 'hyperbolic,' masculinity (Bergmann 157).[28] It is important to emphasize, she is not confused about her gender assignment; she is aware of the fact that she is a daughter, a woman, and regularly uses feminine adjectives to describe herself. To Strother, 'Gila did not want necessarily to be a man, but rather to be *herself*, a unique hybrid of male and female characteristics, without having to give up either of her two sides' (164). In contemporary terms, she can be seen as transgender, or gender queer. That she becomes a serial killer in Act Three places her discomfortingly in a genealogy of representation that pathologizes the 'trans' or gender non-conforming, including such iconic psychopaths and murderers as Norman Bates, the transvestite-murderer in Alfred Hitchcock's *Psycho* (1960), and Buffalo Bill, the sex-change serial killer in Jonathan Demme's *The Silence of the Lambs* (1991).[29] As a butch woman who desires other women, she can also readily be placed alongside, according to Bergmann, other pathological lesbian-killers of recent cinematic vintage – the prototypical 'psycho queer' seen in movies like *Basic Instinct* (1992), *Heavenly Creatures* (1994), and *Butterfly Kiss* (1995) (154). Of course, Gila differs from some of these pathological queers in that she is the tragic protagonist. She is not born to murder but rather ends up murdering due to circumstances placed upon her, which set her on a collision course with both the Captain and everything in her world.

The scenes with the Captain comprise a relatively small portion of *Mountain Girl*. In this respect, the episodic quality of the play serves a purpose. Each episode reinforces how Gila is at odds with everything around her. Her world is laced with threat and menace. The villagers who celebrate her in her first entrance do so with normalizing language that celebrates her beauty, her suitability for marriage, and her fecundity. Do we read irony into

---

28 Bergmann argues that her gender transgression is accepted locally, and encouraged by her father, until the arrival of the Captain, who strips her of masculinity.

29 See Shelley for other examples, including *Myra Breckenridge* and *Rocky Horror Picture Show*.

this? Even if the adulation is earnest, their words of celebration and adoration exert social pressure to live up to a role prescribed for women. Similarly, her amiable friend Mingo also functions antagonistically. He loves her and wants her to be his wife, and she has fend him off at the start of Act Two, when he corners her in a remote stretch of countryside. She seems to handle him comfortably and confidently, and the scene is treated as comedy, but the long string of misogynistic invectives he hurls at her after being rejected darkly suggests the heteronormative pressures he represents, and perhaps sets her up to accept more readily the Captain's marriage proposal in the subsequent scene. That Mingo is the clown figure in this play further emphasizes the incongruity of these episodes, as well as distancing him from his *gracioso* namesake, Mengo, in *Fuente Ovejuna*.[30] Andrés, much more of the arrogant sexist pig, re-inscribes this pattern of a man who expects Gila to act like a woman. Gila repeatedly humiliates him, first while fencing and then later in a fight provoked by gambling. How easily does she win these battles, and at what cost? Giraldo, Gila's father, can be credited as allowing, even encouraging, her gender non-conformity, but he proves a hypocrite; this same man who mocks the Captain in Act One is ready to sell out his daughter in Act Two when confronted with the carrot and stick of flattery and force. As for Queen Isabella, who Gila admires and loves, she is beyond Gila's reach, unattainable, subject to interruptions and distractions beyond Gila's control, and ultimately readily persuadable by her husband to support the severest form of punishment.[31] Ultimately the King and Queen sit atop the very social order that systematically oppresses Gila – a social order whose many strata and forms are on display throughout the play.

Thus, the Captain, who cruelly shames Gila, is the proverbial tip of the spear for this larger order arrayed against Gila, who, whether through enthusiasm, cockiness, or guilelessness, has come to believe what we know is impossible: that she can become an adult in this world without being pigeonholed into a binary; that she, a commoner, can enter, through marriage to a Carvajal, into corridors of power and influence; and that in these corridors she will have access, directly or indirectly, to the woman she loves, the Queen. These are grandiose fantasies, and she is headed for a fall. Logically, then, the play starts with the Captain's trespass into Gila's household, since he catalyzes the events that will lead her to recognize the impossibility of her situation. While he embodies her social world in

30 See Tropé for more on Mingo.

31 See Tropé for more on how Ferdinand functions in the play.

its most cruel and taunting fashion, it is the collective power of the play's many episodes – ranging from scenes of country life to the highest halls of royal power – that give the play its force and throw Gila into relief as an outcast, whose pathology is imposed upon her socially. *Mountain Girl* is therefore at core neither a history play nor a 'rural honor' play like *Fuente Ovejuna* but rather a series of episodes dramatizing a rebel's struggle against a social order.

Contemporary queer theory illuminates Gila's situation and her extreme response. Neither man nor woman, Gila – though she lacks the language to articulate it – can be seen as struggling with the fact that, as Shelley puts it with respect to trans people, the 'third space is an unavailable social position' (11). Heather Love, in *Looking Backward*, looks at literary models of queerness, whose 'ruined or failed sociality' (22) is defined partly by a 'moment of failed or interrupted connection' (24). *Mountain Girl* can be seen as an epic exploration of failed sociality. Appropriately, each of the first two acts ends with a moment of failure: Gila's failure to command the attention of her beloved queen when the news of the Prince's accident interrupts the bullfight (Act One), and Gila's failure to ascend to a position of social power when the Captain abandons her after sleeping with her (Act Two). Moreover, the fascination she repeatedly exerts on others, particularly the Captain, is akin to the *unheimlich* – Julie Kristeva's 'uncanny strangeness' – that, Shelley argues, citing Tim Dean, 'transpeople often unknowingly provoke … rattling perpetrators' deepest gender fictions, in an encounter that may affectively flood their "ego"' (211). She becomes a phobogenic object; fascinating and desirable, she trans-fixes the gaze, and becomes an object of fear/dread.[32] What Gila laments as the destruction of her honor may also be construed, in modern terms, as queer shame, which Jay Prosser describes as 'a profound grappling with the self's location in the world – a feeling of being out of place, of not being at home in a given situation' (179). Trauma is also an apt term for what Gila experiences; indeed, Bergmann calls her situation 'the trauma of dishonor' (153). Whatever label one puts on Gila and her situation, the Captain's actions make her realize that the world is allied against her, that there is no possible recourse in her world to living life as she wants it. Hence her motivation to such extremity.

In becoming a murderer-monster, Gila can be seen as embracing the ethos called for by Lee Edelman in *No Future* (2004). Edelman argues that queerness must radically 'insist that the future stop here' (31); that only

32 See Shelley 211–12.

by 'shattering narrative temporality' (31) – that is, by resisting the social emphasis on children, procreation, heteronormative family structures, and everything that tends toward a happy ending and social integration – 'the queer comes to figure the bar to every realization of futurity, the resistance ... to every social structure or form' (4). It would have been sufficient, for example, for Gila to choose to avenge her honor by merely taking revenge on the individual who dishonored her. Her decision to kill every man she encounters (even if she occasionally makes exceptions) prefigures Edelman. By murdering not only the guilty but the innocent, she renounces narrative temporality, relinquishing her own future and any possibility of pardon or social reintegration. Indeed, she embraces this role and accepts her fate. Her war, after all, is not just with the Captain but everyone around her. Logically, the only space from which she can realize her commitment to no future is outside the space of society, in the sierra, from which she takes her epithet that gives name to the play.

The Captain

The Captain has been compared to Tirso de Molina's Don Juan Tenorio, as well as to military commanders from other rural honor plays.[33] However, just as it would be unwise to read Gila as just another manifestation of the *mujer varonil*, so too would it be misleading to see the Captain as just another villainous *comedia* womanizer who thrives on abusing his power and dishonoring women. He is not a serial mocker and humiliator of women like Don Juan. He is not a predator like the Commander in *Fuente Ovejuna*. Nor does he incite rebellion against legitimate monarchs, as the Commander does. Neither is he an opportunist like Don Álvaro in Calderón de la Barca's *The Mayor of Zalamea*, who uses the opportunity to lodge in a peasant's house for the express purpose of dishonoring his daughter. Nor do all his actions stem from pursuit of a woman with whom he is obsessed, like the Commander in Lope's *Peribáñez*, whose first moment of consciousness in the play is the moment he set his eyes on Casilda. Indeed, as Vélez presents the Captain in the opening scene of the play, his actions are, at least from his own point of view, justifiable. He is in town at the express command of the King and Queen so he can muster troops for the war against the Moors in Granada. It is understandable that he chooses Giraldo's house as his headquarters, given that it is the largest and wealthiest one in town. Yet he immediately finds himself in conflict with this defiant man who refuses

33 For the Don Juan analogy, see Rodríguez Cepada in his edition of the play.

this demand in particularly brazen terms. The opening scene, then, paints a conflict between two proud, stubborn men. It also begs the question: what underlies Giraldo's fierce resistance to the Captain's request? Yes, the Captain is arrogant and disrespectful, but he also seems guilty of some sin not readily discernible in the circumstances.

Gila, shortly after entering and encountering the Captain, names the sin when she taunts him with '*Que fanfarrón jodío*!' (v. 376), which can most literally be translated as 'What a boastful Jew!' She does not mean that he is literally Jewish. Rather, she is impugning him as a New Christian, of dubious heritage. With the exception of Otero-Torres (1997), this dimension of *Mountain Girl* has gone entirely unremarked in modern critical reception of the play; it also is a dimension that distinguishes it from other commander vs. *pueblo* plays of the era.[34] While it could be argued that Gila's line is a commonplace throwaway insult, I would argue that it signals the Captain's status in a way that explains a lot about the play, including the villagers' vicious response to him in Act One, as well as Giraldo's claim to be satisfied by the Captain's family background when he accepts him as son-in-law in Act Two. Why would this background be under suspicion in the first place?[35]

Gila and Giraldo defy the Captain not because his orders are unreasonable but because of his bloodline, something perceptible to them – and to audiences of 1613 – because of his name 'Carvajal.' The Carvajals, as has been noted above, were an illustrious clan in Plasencia and western Spain, some of whom gained considerable fame in service to the church and state, including a number who figured prominently in the conquest of America. Lorenzo Galíndez de Carvajal (1472–c. 1528), for example, was an important chronicler and court official for Ferdinand and Isabella, and later to Charles V. Luis de Carvajal (c. 1537–1591) was governor of the province of Nuevo León, in New Spain (today, Mexico). One can find historical Carvajals in other *comedias* of the time, including Tirso's *La prudencia en la mujer* and *Trilogía de los Pizarros.* (The latter features Francisco de Carvajal, an early-16th-century conquistador of the Andes.) However, there was also a tainted side to the name. Luis de Carvajal's nephew, Luis Rodríguez de Carvajal, for example, was not only a New Christian but apparently a crypto-Jew, practicing his religion in secret. He was arrested in 1590 in Mexico City and subjected to an auto-da-fe. His second arrest, in 1595,

34 See Otero-Torres (1997), 134–35, for more on the implications of the Captain as Jew.

35 My translation of the line in this version, "You arrogant Jew-blooded bastard," encompasses these various implications.

led to his being sentenced to death along with his mother and sisters.[36] A Plasencia Carvajal, Don Lorenzo de Córdoba y Carvajal, was found to have tainted bloodlines when he applied for a church office in 1563, though these bloodlines were not Jewish in origin and ultimately did not prevent him from being granted the office: the prestige of his connections overrode the investigation's conclusions that he was part *mulato*.[37] Roger Luis Martinez has done meticulous research into the ascendancy of the Plasencia Carvajals, and discovered that while the family itself could trace its heritage to Old Christians of northern Spain, they readily established a network of alliances and intermarriages with the *converso* Santa María family in the 15th century. They provide one of the last examples of the cordial and constructive *convivencia* (living together in toleration) that defined many multi-religious towns of late medieval Castile. This was particularly true of Plasencia, which into the late 1300s had a Jewish plurality.[38] To this day, Carvajal is a name found in the Judeo-Spanish (Sephardic) diaspora.[39] The town of Plasencia, the family of Carvajal – these were names that thus bore the imprint of New Christian lineage for audiences in 1613, thereby helping to explain Giraldo and Gila's contempt for the Captain in the opening scenes of the play.

To the extent that the Captain functions as the play's salient antagonist, it is easy to see the play itself as a manifestation of populist anti-Semitism, though ironically written by a playwright who himself had Jewish ancestors – and who, it could be argued, seeks to legitimize himself by making this 'boastful Jew' the villain. I would expand upon this theme from a slightly different angle and argue that the play posits a confrontation between two gender non-normative characters: Gila, a masculine woman, and the Captain, a feminine man. To read the Captain as Jewish is to read him, in his context, as feminized. Such is the argument made by Otero-Torres (1997), citing Louise Mirrer, whose work reveals how Jews were feminized in medieval Spanish culture. Generally represented as lacking masculine strength, this discourse was part of a much larger and persistent tradition of feminizing Jewish men (for example, rumor had it that Jewish men menstruated[40]) that

36 See Perelis for a full accounting.

37 See Moner for a full accounting of this investigation.

38 See Martinez for his extensive, in-depth excavation of the Carvajals and their alliances in Plasencia.

39 See Doreen Carvajal's 2014 article in the *New York Times*, for example.

40 See Lee 105, for example.

persists to this day. To the extent that Gila acts like a man in the opening act, the Captain acts like a woman, allowing himself to be symbolically castrated by Gila in public, driven out of town at phallic rifle point. He does so with barely a whimper, in contrast to the arrogance and taunting of *Fuente*'s Commander, for example, who, even when facing Frondoso's crossbow, dares his young rival to use it. The Captain comes across as strangely passive and helpless in this initial confrontation with Gila. Indeed, he is infatuated with her: her threat of violence against him leads him to confess, in the play's first soliloquy, his love for Gila. According to the stereotypical binary, he has consensually played the woman's role in this spectacle that is both his humiliation and seduction, revealing himself as a surprisingly vulnerable and lonely figure for someone who should be wielding authority in the town. His useless tassled spear suggests his weakness as well. Tellingly, his initial impulses are not to revenge, but to love. It is only when his military buddy, Don García – the play's primary voice of machismo and casual misogyny – shows up, that the Captain proposes the need to burn down the town in revenge. Even so, Don García chides him for his softness and patience. I would argue that it is therefore to rectify his masculinity in the eyes of other men of his social milieu that the Captain starts scheming his revenge. By the time he re-enters in Act Two, he is committed to playing this role and achieving this rectification.

Vélez thus gives us a quality of tragedy in the Captain as well, whose need to prove his masculinity – on shaky ground because of his status as New Christian – drives him to humiliate Gila in a way that leads to his own destruction. He becomes both perpetrator of the oppressive social order that runs Gila through the gauntlet over the course of the play, and also another example, like Gila, of someone non-normative whose Desire (for Gila) is sacrificed to the Law. His presence also potentially makes the play queer.

Textual and Stage History

The Mountain Girl from La Vera was never published in its day. Instead, it survives in autograph (that is, a manuscript in the author's own hand) in the National Library of Madrid. The manuscript is fascinating. It is signed by the author, with coded rubrics at the top of each act that list the names of his family. One stage direction and a number of annotations specify that Vélez sees the famed actress Jusepa Vaca as playing Gila, suggesting she was important to his development of the character, if not inseparable from his conception of it. The manuscript also has numerous indications, put there either by the author himself or the theater company that owned the script (presumably, Vaca's), of how the play might have been trimmed for performance.

408 verses, or 12.3% of the play, are indicated for cutting in some way.[41] Many of the cuts are minor. They shape speeches, edit scenes, so as to make them more economical, direct. A few seem designed to avoid unintentional comedy or awkwardness. Many of the cuts, though, are ideological in nature. For example, they minimize the homoerotic valence in Gila's speech to Isabella near the end of Act One, taking out, for example, the line when she pointedly says she is '*enamorada*' (in love with) the Queen. Other deletions are to sections of dialogue which place royalty in a less than flattering light, such as Mingo's story in Act Two about the queen who cuckolds her husband by bedding a dwarf, as well as Ferdinand and Isabella's entire scene in Act Three in which the Queen expresses jealousy over Gila. Finally, most dramatically, the end of the play is significantly truncated. Madalena and Pascuala's description of the stirring tableau of Gila's death is eliminated, as well as, presumably, the tableau itself. Instead, the cut version of the script jumps from Gila's biting off of her father's ear to Rodrigo's final words. The resulting end is flatter, less interesting: it pushes the play away from complex tragedy and toward moralizing melodrama.[42] The net result of all these potential cuts, as Peale has persuasively argued, is a performance text that is far more orthodox and conventional than the complete play.[43]

We know that Vaca performed the role of Gila in 1614 in Alba de Tormes, with the theatre company managed by her husband Juan de Morales, and so Vélez did succeed in landing his script with the stage sensation who would do it justice. The demands of the role are extraordinary. Gila is on stage for most of the play. The actress playing her has to have some sort of stage presence or charisma that makes her credible and compelling in both comic and tragic moments. She has to be able to handle rifles with ease, ride horses with confidence, fence with skill, and show some flair as a bullfighter. She has to move agilely across multiple stage levels, not to

41 These numbers come from Peale's *Estudio* (2002). The 'might' is an important caveat. We do not know how much of the proposed cuts were actually implemented in performance. They may suggest a range of possible cuts to choose from, depending on circumstance.

42 See Peale's *Estudio*, 58–60, for a detailed consideration of how the cuts impact the end of the play.

43 Both Bolaños (2001) and Peale (2002) offer excellent blow-by-blow analysis of the cuts and their impact.

mention subdue men physically. Failure for the performer to be persuasive in these performances is tantamount to failing in the role.

Vaca was one of the few performers in Spain, female or male, who had these chops. She was celebrated for her *mujeres varoniles* and was also known as a crack comedienne. Offstage, her life was tinged with scandal and rumor. Satirists and commentators cruelly mocked her supposed lack of chastity; her husband, Morales, was also written about as a pathetic cuckold or willing pimp.[44]

Boyle argues that the play superimposes Vaca onto the body of Gila. Both Vaca and Gila, after all, are objects of public fascination: 'unruly women' who serve as both cautionary models and exemplars of achievement (80). Martín (2008) foregrounds the erotic in her consideration of Vaca/Gila, arguing that 'the role of Gila was written specifically to exploit Vaca's theatrical and erotic talents' (163). From the start, the play is full of 'spectacular appearances by Gila/Jusepa' that 'fuse and never separate eroticism and violence' (165), from her feats of horsemanship (explicitly showing off her legs and feet) to the final tableau of her arrow-ridden corpse – a tableau that that would have required Vaca to be partially undressed. For Boyle, Vaca shadows Gila as an auto-da-fe penitent, consigned to a spectacle of penitence; for Martín, Vaca underscores Gila as ritual scapegoat, brutally punished for defying community norms. If we presume that Morales played the Captain, then his body as cuckolded husband/failed man also shadows the play. He would have been, after all, subjected to the ultimate on-stage humiliation: avenged and destroyed by his very own wife before the eyes of thousands of spectators.[45]

Mountain Girl was first published in 1916, in an edition by Menéndez Pidal. Three critical editions have appeared more recently: Enrique Rodríguez Cepada (1967), Piedad Bolaños (2001), and William R. Manson and C. George Peale (2002). I have been able to find only two examples of professional performances of the play since 1614. One is the 2004 production by the Compañía Nacional de Teatro Clasico (CNTC), who did it at Madrid's Teatro Pavón, directed by Maria Ruiz and starring Mía Esteve, in an adaptation by Luis Landero. In publicity materials prepared for the production, Landero compares Gila to great unconventional female characters – Ibsen's Nora, Strindberg's Miss Julie, Flaubert's Madame Bovary. Ruiz called it: 'Una

44 See Reyes Peña for excellent documentation of this discourse about Vaca.

45 Vaca outlived her husband and went on to inherit his company. She founded a guild for actors in 1631 and lived until 1653.

obra difícil, o al menos así me lo parece, por el talento de su autor para lo grotesco y la abrupta ruptura de situaciones, que constituyen a la vez algunas de sus mejores virtudes.'[46] ('A difficult work, or at least so it seems to me, due to its author's talent for the grotesque, for abrupt ruptures in situations, which at the same time count as some of its greatest virtues.') Much more recently, in September 2017, LaBotiKa Teatro in Cáceres, Spain (not far from Plasencia) debuted their own adaptation, which featured original music. In respect to Gila, they promised: 'La hemos quitado el polvo y el olor de naftalina para convertirla en una auténtica heroína del Siglo de Oro, que traspasa como mujer los límites morales y sociales establecidos'[47] ('We have rid her of her dust and smell of mothballs in order to transform her into an authentic heroine of the Golden Age, who as a woman transgresses established moral and social boundaries.')

The University of Massachusetts Department of Theater will debut my translation, under the name *Wild Thing*, in February 2019, under the direction of my colleague and collaborator Gina Kaufmann. Our version will also cut the script down to about 90 minutes. We are in preliminary conversation about how to cast the play as I write these words.

A Note on the Translation

As a theater practitioner, I have created this translation with an ear for orality: how it speaks, how it sounds, how it might work in the voices and bodies of actors today. The side-by-side bilingual format of this series inspires me with the hope that my version, while containing every idea in Vélez's play, can stand on its own, facing it across the page as an equal, different from but not subordinate to the original. Think of it as a sibling that has adapted itself to thrive in another set of circumstances rather than a distant mirror of something more authentic.

Comedias deploy multiple verse forms. At their heart, however, are *redondillas* and *romance*: poetic forms of four-line stanzas, each line containing eight syllables and four beats. They result in plays that are light and vibrant, that move swiftly and musically. Thoughts tumble out quickly, lines jab rapidly back and forth as characters spar with each other. 85% of the lines in *Mountain Girl* are in *redondillas, romance*, or similar eight-syllable forms. While I have not distinguished among these forms in rendering

46 'La Serrana' program notes.
47 'La Serrana … mujer libre' article.

the play into English, I have committed myself to keeping the line length short for this same 85% of the play, using lines of 7–9 syllables, generally speak-able in four beats. I have tried to maintain attention to the integrity of the line as a unit of thought meaning. Unlike Vélez's original, my lines are not metered, nor do they rhyme in any regular fashion. However, I have woven internal rhyme (and some end rhyme) into my rhetoric whenever the opportunity presented itself without a risk of twisting the meaning. Indeed, I work hard never to sacrifice meaning for a turn of phrase, a goal made attainable by liberation from meter and rhyme. I take confidence from translators like Laurence Boswell, Catherine Boyle, and David Johnston who have used similar strategies to wonderful results, all of which have borne great fruit on stage.

Golden Age playwrights often resorted to 'Italianate' verse forms (10–12 syllables per line) for variety or contrast. These longer lines make up a minority of lines in a given play. In the case of *Mountain Girl*, the remaining 15% of the verses are in some variety of these forms. The effect is graver, denser, more formal and stately, and Vélez accordingly uses them for most of the scenes with Ferdinand and Isabella, as well as the courtly-esque negotiations in Act Two between Giraldo, the Captain, and Gila. My translation honors the longer line length in the same 15% of the play for the same intended purpose.

The villagers in the play speak, somewhat inconsistently, in a stereotypical rural dialect that also marks them regionally as being from western Spain. This dialect comes across mostly in non-standard word choices – for example, *hendo* for *haciendo* (doing). At the same time, most of these characters – and certainly Gila and Giraldo – are capable of sustaining more standardized (indeed, highly eloquent) diction for long stretches of time. In my translation, I have elected not to reproduce any conspicuous ruralisms, which would require assigning the characters some milieu (Appalachia? Highland Scotland?) that ultimately would distract or mislead. Rather, I hope more subtle choices in register help to convey the play's varied linguistic landscape.

I am indebted to C. George Peale, for generously allowing the University of Liverpool Press to publish his and William R. Manson's authoritative Spanish edition opposite my translation. It has been my indispensable guide. Everything on the left-hand is the work of their editorial prowess. That said, the English on the right contains some editorial choices of my own, including indications of scene breaks, as well as the settings for these scenes. I have also clarified and in many cases repositioned stage directions. (Stage directions are often anticipatory in the manuscript, placed a few lines before the action logically occurs, suggesting that they were meant to give the actors a little bit of lead time with their cues.) Anything not in the original manuscript is indicated in the translation by either () or [], the former denoting where I have incorporated the work of former editors and the latter indicating my own editorial additions. I have also, through the use of brackets, indicated which sections of the manuscript are set aside for potential omission. These places are clearly noted. Finally, I have standardized and modernized the spelling of some characters' names.

As for my end notes, they owe a great debt to Manson and Peale and to Piedad Bolaños. I have specifically acknowledged this debt only when the annotation involved a more specialized level of research. Also, frequently, I have incorporated the endnote's gloss into the spoken text, assuming modern listeners need to hear this context to grasp an implication in a way that Vélez's audiences did not.

La Serrana de la Vera is remarkably vibrant and accessible play, even for its time. At least that's how I see it. I hope these qualities come across in *The Mountain Girl of La Vera.*

BIBLIOGRAPHY

Bergman, Emilie L. 'Women Tame and Untamed: Two Dutiful Daughters in the *Romance de la doncella guerrera* and Luis Vélez de Guevara's *La serrana de la Vera*.' In *Shakespeare and the Spanish Comedia: Translation, Interpretation, Performance: Essays in Honor of Susan Fischer.* Ed. Barbara Mujica. Lewisburg, PA: Bucknell UP, 2013, 149–64.

Bolaños, Piedad. 'Deconstrucción de arquéticos trafictionales: voz, traje y ademanes en *El rey naciendo mujer* de Luis Vélez de Guevara.' In *Las mujeres en la sociedad española del Siglo de Oro: Ficción teatral y realidad histórica.* Eds Juan Antonio Martínez Berbel and Roberto Castilla Pérez. Granada: U. of Granada, 1998, 57–79.

Bolaños, Piedad. Introducción. In *La serrana de la Vera*. Ed. Piedad Bolaños. Madrid: Clásicos Castalia, 2001, 9–73.

Boyle, Margaret E. *Unruly Women: Performance, Penitence, and Punishment in Early Modern Spain.* Toronto: U of Toronto P, 2014.

Bradbury, Gail. 'Irregular Sexuality in the Spanish Comedia.' *MLR* 76 (1981), 566–80.

Carvajal, Doreen. 'In Spain, a Family Reunion, Centuries Later.' *NY Times* 4 April 2014.

Cid Martínez, Jesús Antonio. 'Romances en Garganta la Olla.' *RDTP* 30 (1974), 476–527.

Davies, Gareth. 'Luis Velez de Guevara and Court Life.' In *Antigüedad y actualidad de Luis Vélez de Guevara.* Ed. C. George Peale. Purdue U Monographs. Philadelphia: John Benjamins Publishing, 1983, 13–38.

Delpech, Francois. 'La leyenda de la serrana de la Vera: las adaptaciones teatrales.' In *La mujer en el teatro y la novela del siglo XVII: actas del II Coloquio del Grupo de Estudios sobre Teatro Español* (G.E.S.T.E.), Toulouse, 16–17, Noviembre 1978, 23–38.

Edelman, Lee. *No Future: Queer Theory and the Death Drive.* Durham: Duke University Press, 2004.

Gutiérrez Macías, Valeriano. 'La serrana de la Vera en el folklore.' *Revista de Folklore* 92 (1988), 39–43.

Kamen, Henry. *Spain 1469–1714: A Society of Conflict.* Essex, UK: Longman, 1983.

Lee, Christina H. *The Anxiety of Sameness in Early Modern Spain.* Manchester: Manchester UP, 2016.

Love, Heather. *Feeling Backward: Loss and the Politics of Queer History.* Cambridge: Harvard University Press, 2007.

Lundelius, Ruth. 'Paradox and Role Reversal in *La serrana de la Vera.*' In *The Perception of Women in Spanish Theater of the Golden Age*. Eds Anita K. Stoll and Dawn L. Smith. Lewisburg, PA: Bucknell UP, 1991, 220–44.

Mariscal, George. 'Symbolic Capital in the Spanish Comedia.' *Renaissance Drama* 21 (1990), 143–69.

Martín, Adrienne Laskier. *An Erotic Philology of Golden Age Spain*. Nashville: Vanderbilt UP, 2008.

Martín, Adrienne Laskier. 'Onstage/Backstage: Animals in the Golden Age Comedia.' In *A Companion to Early Modern Hispanic Theater*. Ed. Hilaire Kalendorf. Boston: Brill, 2014, 127–44.

Martín Ojeda, Marina and C. George Peale. 'Historiografía, genealogía, y onomástica: la cuestión de judaísmo de Luis Vélez de Guevara.' *Criticón* 129 (2017), 7–22.

Martinez, Roger Luis. 'From Sword to Seal: The Ascent of the Carvajal Family in Spain (1391-1516).' Unpublished dissertation. U of Texas at Austin, 2008.

McKendrick, Malveena. *Woman and Society in the Spanish Drama of the Golden Age: A Study of the Mujer Varonil*. Cambridge: Cambridge UP, 1974.

Meadows, Harrison. 'Staging Gender Transgression and Transphobia in Hispanic Classical Theater.' Unpublished paper. American Society for Theatre Research (ASTR) Conference. Minneapolis, November 2016.

Mirrer, Louise. 'Representing "Other" Men: Muslims, Jews, and Masculine Ideals in Medieval Castilian Epic and Ballad.' *Medieval Masculinities: Regarding Men in the Middle Ages.* Ed. Clare A. Lees. Minneapolis: U. of Minnesota, 1994, 169–86.

Moner, Baltasar Cuart. 'La sombra del arcediano: El linaje oculto de Don Lorenzo Galíndez de Carvajal.' *Studia Historica* 15 (1996), 135–78.

Morreale, Margherita. 'Apuntaciones para el estudio del tema de la serrana en dos comedias de Luis Velez de Guevara.' In *Antigüedad y actualidad de Luis Vélez de Guevara.* Ed. C. George Peale. Purdue U Monographs. Philadelphia: John Benjamins Publishing, 1983, 104–10.

Otero-Torres, Dámaris M. 'Gila Giraldo y Juespa Vaca: La poética del castigo y el fracas commercial en *La serrana de la Vera.*' In *A Society on Stage: Essays on Spanish Golden Age Drama.* Eds. Edward Friedman, H. Manrari, D. Miller. U Press of the South, 1998, 173–81.

Otero-Torres, Dámaris M. 'Historia, ortodoxía y praxis teatral: el homoeroticsimo femenino en *La serrana de la Vera.*' *El escritor y la escena* 5 (1997), 131–39.

Palacios Diazceballos, Carolina. '*La Serrana de la Vera* de Velez de Guevara y el romanticismo incipiente.' *Romance Notes* 47.3 (2007), 237–44.

Parr, James A. 'Some Remarks on Tragedy and on Velez as a Tragedian (A Response to Professor Whitby).' In *Antigüedad y actualidad de Luis Vélez de Guevara.* Ed. C. George Peale. Purdue U Monographs. Philadelphia: John Benjamins Publishing, 1983, 137–43.

Parr, James A. and Lourdes Albuixech. Estudio introductorio. In *La Serrana de la*

Vera. Eds William R. Manson and C. George Peale. Newark, DE: Juan de la Cuesta, 2002, 15–39.

Peale, C. George. 'El acto I de *La Serrana de la Vera* de Vélez de Guevara: hacia una poetica del bufón.' *El escritor y la escena* 5 (1997), 141–58.

Peale, C. George. Estudio bibliográfico y métrico. In *La Serrana de la Vera*. Eds William R. Manson and C. George Peale. Newark, DE: Juan de la Cuesta, 2002, 41–62.

Perelis, Ronnie. *Narratives from the Sephardic Atlantic*. Bloomington: Indiana UP, 2016.

Profeti, Maria Grazia. 'Emisor y receptores: Luis Velez de Guevara y el enfoque critico.' In *Antigüedad y actualidad de Luis Vélez de Guevara*. Ed. C. George Peale. Purdue U Monographs. Philadelphia: John Benjamins Publishing, 1983, 1–12.

Prosser, Jay. *Second Skins: The Body Narratives of Transsexuality*. New York: Columbia University Press.

Reyes Peña, Mercedes de los. 'En torno a la actriz Juespa Vaca.' In *Las mujeres en la sociedad española del Siglo de Oro: Ficción teatral y realidad histórica*. Eds Juan Antonio Martínez Berbel and Roberto Castilla Pérez. Granada: U. of Granada, 1998, 81–114.

Rodríguez Cepada, Enrique. Estudio, In *La serrana de la Vera*. Ed. Enrique Ródrigiez Cepada. Madrid: Ediciones Alcala, 1967, 9–45

Rossi, Teresa M. 'El lenguaje paremilogico de los campesinos en *La serrana de la Vera* de Luis Velez de Guevara.' In *Antigüedad y actualidad de Luis Vélez de Guevara*. Ed. C. George Peale. Purdue U Monographs. Philadelphia: John Benjamins Publishing, 1983, 89–103.

'"La Serrana de la Vera, mujer libre y fiera" con LaBotiKa.' *El Periodico Extremadura*. 22 September, 2017. http://www.elperiodicoextremadura.com/noticias/caceres/la-serrana-vera-mujer-libre-fiera-labotika_1041352.html

'*La Serrana de la Vera* de Luis Velez de Guevara.' Program notes from 2004 CNTC production. http://www.piornal.net/cajondesastre/seraserranavera.htm

Shelley, Christopher. *Transpeople: Repudiation, Trauma, Healing*. Toronto: University of Toronto Press, 2008.

Silió, Elisa. 'La Compañía de Teatro Clásico rescata una obra de Vélez de Guevara.' *El País* 25 March 2004.

Strother, Darci L. 'Constructing a Goddess: Gila's Role in Vélez de Guevara's *La serrana de la Vera*. In *A Star-crossed Golden Age: Myth and the Spanish Comedia*. Ed. Frederick de Armas. Lewisburg, PA: Bucknell UP, 1998, 162–78.

Stroud, Matthew D. *Plot Twists and Critical Turns: Queer Approaches to Early Modern Spanish Theater.* Lewisburg, PA: Bucknell UP, 2007.

Stroud, Matthew D. 'The Resocialization of the Mujer Varonil in Three Plays by Vélez. In *Antigüedad y actualidad de Luis Vélez de Guevara*. Ed. C. George Peale. Purdue U Monographs. Philadelphia: John Benjamins Publishing, 1983, 111–26.

Sullivan, Henry W. 'Lacan and Tragic Drama in the Golden Age of Spain.' In *A Companion to Early Modern Hispanic Theater*. Ed. Hilaire Kalendorf. Boston: Brill, 2014, 311–35.

Tropé, Hélène. 'La confrontation du roi, des nobles et des paysans dans *La serrana de la Vera* de Luis Vélez de Guevara. *Études epistéme* 14 (2008), 19–30.

Urzáiz Tortajada, Hector. Introducción. In *Luis Velez de Guevara: Teatro Breve*. Madrid: Iberoamericana, 2002, 17–62.

Valladares Reguero, Aurelio. 'Bandolerismo y santidad femininos en el teatro del Siglo de Oro.' In *Las mujeres en la sociedad española del Siglo de Oro: Ficción teatral y realidad histórica*. Eds Juan Antonio Martínez Berbel and Roberto Castilla Pérez. Granada: U. of Granada, 1998, 395–428.

Vega, Lope. *La serrana de la Vera*. In *Obras escogidas*. Volume III. Madrid: Aguilar, 1962, 1295–328.

Vélez de Guevara, Luis. *La serrana de la Vera*. Ed. Enrique Ródrigiez Cepada. Madrid: Ediciones Alcala, 1967.

Vélez de Guevara, Luis. *La serrana de la Vera*. Ed. Piedad Bolaños. Madrid: Clásicos Castalia, 2001.

Vélez de Guevara, Luis. *La Serrana de la Vera*. Eds William R. Manson and C. George Peale. Newark, DE: Juan de la Cuesta, 2002.

Whitby, William. 'Some Thoughts on Velez as Tragedian.' In *Antigüedad y actualidad de Luis Vélez de Guevara*. Ed. C. George Peale. Purdue U Monographs. Philadelphia: John Benjamins Publishing, 1983, 127–36.

Yovel, Yirmiyahu. *The Other Within: The Marranos*. Princeton: Princeton UP, 2009.

Ziomek, Henryk and Ann N. Hughes. Introductory materials. *El cerro de Roma por el rey Desiderio: A Critical Edition*. Kassel: Edition Reichenberger, 1992, 1–44.

LA SERRANA DE LA VERA

THE MOUNTAIN GIRL FROM LA VERA

Para la señora Jusepa Vaca

PERSONAS

GIRALDO, labrador viejo
DON JUAN DE CARVAJAL, alcalde de la Hermandad
GILA, la serrana
MINGO, gracioso
PASCUAL
VICENTE
LLORENTE
BRAS
DON GARCÍA, alférez
DOS DE PLASENCIA
VENDEDORES
ANDRÉS, bravo
GERÓNIMO, bravo
MADALENA
DOÑA ISABEL, reina de Castilla y León
DON FERNANDO, rey de Aragón
DON NUÑO, criado del rey
DON LUCAS, CAPITÁN
DON RODRIGO GIRÓN, el maestre de Calatrava
CABO DE ESCUADRA
PASCUALA, niña
SARGENTO
CAMINANTE
AGUADOR
MÚSICOS
CUADRILLEROS

Jesús María Josef
Luis Úrsola Francisco Juan Antonio

For Señora Jusepa Vaca[1]

CHARACTERS[2]

GIRALDO, elderly villager; Gila's father
CAPTAIN DON LUCAS DE CARVAJAL[3]
GILA, the *serrana* or 'mountain girl'
MINGO, villager; *gracioso* or comic figure
PASCUAL, villager
VICENTE, villager
LLORENTE, villager
BRAS, villager
DON GARCÍA, lieutenant
TWO PEOPLE at the Plasencia fiesta
VARIOUS VENDORS at the Plasencia fiesta
FENCING MASTER
PERICO, his assistant
ANDRÉS, *bravo* or roughneck
GERÓNIMO, *bravo* or roughneck
MADALENA, villager; Gila's cousin
QUEEN ISABELLA of Castile and Leon
KING FERDINAND of Aragon[4]
DON NUÑO, royal servant
DON RODRIGO GIRÓN, Master of Calatrava[5]
CORPORAL
PASCUALA, little girl
VARIOUS TROOP MEMBERS of the Holy Brotherhood
DON JUAN DE CARVAJAL, HEAD of the Holy Brotherhood

Jesús María Josef[6]
Luis Úrsola Francisco Juan Antonio[7]

ACTO PRIMERO

GIRALDO, labrador viejo, rico, y DON LUCAS DE CARVAJAL, capitán, con su jineta, y en cuerpo, muy galán, y dice GIRALDO:

GIRALDO Si sois capitán del Rey,
seldo muy enhorabuena,
que no me puede dar pena
el serville a toda ley,
pero en mi casa jamás
se alojó nadie, y sospecho
que el Consejo no lo ha hecho,
ni el Alcalde.

CAPITÁN ¿El Rey no es más?

GIRALDO ¿Quién lo niega? Mas aquí
ellos al Rey representan,
y nunca mi casa afrentan,
si puede decirse así,
con hacerla alojamiento.

CAPITÁN ¿Sois hidalgo?

GIRALDO No, señor,
pero soy un labrador
con honrado nacimiento,
cristiano viejo y honrado,
que nosotros no pudimos
escoger cuando nacimos
la nobleza ni el estado.
Que a fe que, a ser en mi mano,
y a quererlo también Dios,
naciera mejor que vos.

CAPITÁN ¡Qué filósofo villano!

GIRALDO Más a espacio, si es posible,
señor Capitan, que a fe
que, aunque estoy viejo, sabré
tener valor invencible
para no dejar que vos
me ofendáis.

ACT ONE

[Act One, Scene 1. The village of Garganta la Olla.][8]

Enter Giraldo, a wealthy old villager, and Captain Don Lucas de Carvajal. The Captain, simply attired, cuts a striking figure with his tasseled spear and sash.[9]

GIRALDO If you are the King's captain,[10]
You are most welcome here:
It gives me no displeasure to
Serve you as law requires.
But never before has any man
Demanded my house to quarter soldiers.
This can't be at the orders of
The Mayor or Village Council.
CAPTAIN Isn't the King above them both?
GIRALDO Who denies it? But in this village,
They represent the King.
Never would they insult my house –
If I may dare say so myself –
By offering it to soldiers.
CAPTAIN So you're a nobleman?[11]
GIRALDO No, señor,
But I am a villager of
Honored birth and Christian blood.
We cannot choose the time we're born,
Or our rank or social worth,
But I swear, had I the choice,
Or had God above seen fit,
I could be the one higher born.
CAPTAIN The peasant dog's a philosopher!
GIRALDO Get a hold of yourself, señor.
I may be old, but I swear I'll find
The nerve to stop this insult.

CAPITÁN ¿No sois villano?
GIRALDO Hombre soy humilde y llano,
mas villano no, por Dios,
sino es porque vivo en villa,
que villano es el que intenta
a traición muerte o afrenta.
Hombres buenos en Castilla
sus reyes nos han llamado,
y los que son hombres buenos,
de ese nombre están ajenos.
Pero habláis como soldado,
y aun como soldado mozo
que, a ser más viejo, en efeto,
tratara con mas respeto
estas canas vuestro bozo.
CAPITÁN Los que nobles han nacido
servicios no han menester
con los reyes para ser
lo que otros han merecido
cuando muchos les han hecho,
que en impresas semejantes
sirvieron por ellos antes
con más que invencible pecho
sus nobles antepasados,
y Plasencia de los míos
conoce muy bien los bríos
que en ella están sepultados,
aunque han fama inmortal,
que, de los Carvajales,
sirviendo como leales
a la corona real,
y como muy valerosos
en Portugal y en Castilla,
dan muestras en su capilla
mil trofeos generosos.
Y así los Reyes –que guarde
mil siglos, amén, el Cielo
en el castellano suelo–,

CAPTAIN So you're not a peasant dog?
GIRALDO I am a plain and humble man,
But by God! – I am no dog.
Perhaps I live in what you'd call
A base, unpleasant village
But this small place in no way makes me
A base, unpleasant peasant,
A villain or a dog.[12]
A dog is a man who's treacherous,
Who insults others, who takes their lives.
Here in Castile, the King and Queen
Have declared us rural folk
To be good and decent men,
And a good man is no dog.
But you speak like a soldier, señor,
And what's more, a very young one.
That fuzz upon your upper lip
Should pay respect to these gray locks.
CAPTAIN Those who spring from noble stock
Need no special royal decree
To receive the respect that's due them.
The extraordinary feats
Of their noble ancestors
Vouch for them at every instant.
Mine are from Plasencia:
That city knows their spirit well,
It knows the name of Carvajal,
It shall know that name forever –
A name that's loyally served the crown,
A name whose countless acts of courage
Are hallowed in holy chapels
Across Portugal and Castile.
Know this then: the King and Queen –
May God protect them forever! –

de quien son haciendo alarde,
    para la famosa guerra
de Granada me han nombrado
por capitán, y me han dado
patente para mi tierra
    por mayor merced. Y así
en toda la Vera puedo
hacer gente, y hoy me quedo
a tocar cajas aquí
    y a levantar la bandera,
porque en Plasencia querría
entrar ya con compañía
de la gente de la Vera,
    porque es grande gusto entrar
por su patria tan honrado
el que salió a ser soldado.
Y por ser tan buen lugar
    Garganta la Olla, quise
que tenga principio en él,
y en vuestra casa, pues de él
no hay nadie que no me avise
    que es la mejor, y sois vos
el más rico del lugar,
y es buen puesto para estar
la bandera.

GIRALDO ¡Guárdeos Dios
    por la merced que me hacéis!
Pero yo os agradeciera,
en lo que posible fuera,
mucho más que lo escuséis,
    y os serviré desde aquí
en cuanto queráis mandarme.

CAPITÁN Si he de llegar a enfadarme,
escusaldo vos.

GIRALDO A mí
    nunca me echaron soldados,
y no los he de tener.

Are mustering soldiers for our
Famed campaign against Granada.[13]
They've named me Captain and,
By highest royal favor,
Granted me exclusive patent
Over my homeland, to gather men
Throughout La Vera as I see fit.[14]
I'm here to beat the recruitment drum
And hoist the flag of headquarters.
When I make my grand entrance
In Plasencia's central plaza,
I want to be in the company of
The finest men in La Vera.
What a way to be welcomed home!
Who wouldn't want to leave, a soldier,
And return, honored, a hero?
Garganta la Olla's a fine little village.
I choose it as the launching place
For this historic campaign.
Your house will be its beating heart:
Everyone tells me, it's the finest in town,
And you, the wealthiest man.
What better place to hoist my flag.

GIRALDO May God keep you for this favor
You're intent on showing me!
But I would hold you in the highest
Estimation if you could
Excuse me from this obligation:
I vow to serve you, señor,
In any other way you choose.

CAPTAIN If you intend to test my patience,
Why don't you excuse it yourself?

GIRALDO I've never had to quarter soldiers.
And I will not.

CAPITÁN Esto esta vez ha de ser,
¡por vida del Rey!
GIRALDO Crïados
y vasallos suyos somos,
pero no pienso serviros
en eso.
CAPITÁN Yo sí mediros
con la jineta los lomos,
y hacer a palos aquí
lo que por bien no queréis,
que como encinas daréis
el fruto mejor así.
GIRALDO Idos, señor Capitán,
más a la mano, ¡por Dios!,
que ni encina soy ni vos
sois el paladín Roldán
para mostraros tan fiero
conmigo en mi casa.
CAPITÁN Haré
lo que digo, por la fe
de soldado y caballero.
GIRALDO Pues por la fe de hombre honrado,
que no lo hagáis, que aunque estoy
viejo, padre de hijos soy,
y si el Cielo no me ha dado
varón que pueda volver
vida arrestando y honor
por las ofensas, señor,
que vos me podáis hacer,
una hija me dio el Cïelo
que podré decir que vale
por dos hijos, porque sale
a su padre y a su agüelo,
que fuera de la presencia
hermosa, tan gran valor
tiene, que no hay labrador
en la Vera de Plasencia
que a correr no desafíe,

CAPTAIN This time you will –
I swear by the King himself!
GIRALDO We are your vassals and servants,
But this service, I cannot do.
CAPTAIN I'll measure your ribcage with my spear
And rain down blows until, like an oak,
You drop your finest fruit.
GIRALDO Be gone, señor. But careful.
I am no oak, nor you some Roland.
From an heroic epic of old
To be strutting around so furiously
At the threshold to my home.[15]
CAPTAIN On my word as solider and gentleman,
I intend to do just what I said.
GIRALDO On your word as a man of honor,
May you not do what you just said.
I may be an old man, yes –
But I am also a father,
And though God has not blessed me
With a son who can restore
My honor for this base offense,
He has given me a daughter,
Worth as much as two full-grown sons.
She takes after her father and
Her grandfather before him.
She has a beautiful figure,
But, more so, she has rare courage.
There's no man in all La Vera
Who she doesn't challenge in

a saltar, luchar, tirar
la barra, y en el lugar
no hay ninguno que porfíe
a mostrar valor mayor
en ninguna cosa de estas,
porque de las manifiestas
vitorias de su valor
tienen ya grande experiencia
que es su ardimiento bizarro.
De bueyes, detiene un carro,
de un molino, la violencia.
Corre un caballo mejor
que si en él cosida fuera,
y en medio de la carrera
y de la furia mayor,
que parece que al través
a dar con un monte viene,
suelta el freno y le detiene
con las piernas y los pies.
Esta mañana salió
en uno al monte a cazar,
y casi todo el lugar
tras ella, que la siguió.
Siempre que a caza ha salido,
por verla con la escopeta
cómo los vientos sujeta,
que ningún tiro ha perdido
al vuelo, de tal manera
que no hay ave que la aguarde,
ni todo el furioso alarde
de los brutos.

CAPITÁN No me diera
mucha pesadumbre a mí,
que yo luchara con ella
de buena gana. Y si es bella,
como referís aquí,
y tan diestra en el luchar
como en todo maravilla,

Sprinting, jumping, wrestling,
And hurling the javelin.
In each of these feats she's unsurpassed.
Ask anyone: they've all tasted
Her fierce and fiery spirit.
She stops oxen in their path,
She halts a whirling windmill,
And when she gallops on a horse,
She and the beast are stitched as one.
When at peak of furious gallop
And it seems she's bound to shatter
Against a rocky mountainside,
She drops the reins and brings the beast
To a sudden standstill with
Just her legs and feet.
Why, this very morning she rode off
On exactly such a steed
To go hunting in the mountains,
And almost everyone in town
Trailed behind, as they always do,
Just to watch her with her rifle,
Just to see the way she stifles
The wild wind whipping above.
She never misses a shot.
No bird in the sky can hide from her,
Nor the thunderous herds of beasts
That dwell on the land below.

CAPTAIN It would give me no displeasure to
Wrestle with her for a while,
If she's as pretty as you say.
And if she's so skilled at it too,

con alguna zancadilla
la intentara derribar.

GIRALDO Castigar sabe también
malicias de esa manera.

CAPITÁN Pondráse aquí la bandera,
y después sabremos quién
podrá más de ambos a dos,
que, según la habéis pintado,
si quiere ser mi soldado,
os doy palabra, por Dios,
de darle mi escuadra.

GIRALDO Estáis
de espacio y de buen humor.

(Tocan un atambor.)

CAPITÁN Ya pienso que el atambor,
puesto que vos no gustáis
del cuerpo de guardia aquí,
quiere tomar posesión,
y echar el bando en razón
de mi patente. Y así,
haced… ¿Cómo es vuestra gracia?

GIRALDO Giraldo

CAPITÁN Giraldo amigo,
para todo lo que os digo
sin género de desgracia
apercebir luego luego
lo que fuere necesario.
Y no lo hagáis al contrario,
ya que por bien os lo ruego,
si hacerme queréis favor,
pues no se escusa ya.

GIRALDO Ya viene Gila, y podrá
daros recado, señor.

Suenen relinchos de LABRADORES, y vayan entrando por el patio cantando TODA LA COMPAÑÍA, menos LOS DOS que están en el tablado, con coronas de flores, y UNO con un palo largo y en él metido un pellejo de un lobo con su cabeza, y OTRO con otro de oso de la misma suerte, y OTRO

I'll have to use my very best moves
To pin her to the ground.

GIRALDO She knows how
To punish that kind of cunning.

CAPTAIN My flag will be hoisted here.
We'll see which one of us prevails.
If she is as you describe her,
And wishes to be my soldier,
By God, I give you my word:
She can have my whole squad.

GIRALDO You must be joking.

(Drumbeats.)

CAPTAIN That's the drum.
My company guard arrives
To proclaim my royal patent and
Take possession of your house
Whether you like it or not.
What is your grace's name?

GIRALDO Giraldo

CAPTAIN Giraldo, my friend,
Nothing I've told you has any
Measure of rancor or enmity.
Simply grasp, right here, right now,
What needs to happen, and please
Don't go against my command.
Show me your favor, and understand:
There is no escaping this
Obligation before you.

GIRALDO I hear Gila coming, señor.
She will give you our answer.

The sound of villagers in celebration. They enter the patio of the theater, all of them singing (except the two on stage), crowned with flowers.[16] *One has a large pole with a wolf's skin and head on it. Another has a similar pole, with a bear's head. Another has one with a wild boar's head. Behind them,*

con otro de jabalí.Y luego, detrás, a caballo, GILA, la Serrana de la Vera, vestida a lo serrano, de mujer, con sayuelo y muchas patenas,el cabello tendido, y una montera con plumas, un cuchillo de monte al lado, botín argentado, y puesta una escopeta debajo del caparazón del caballo, y lo que cantan es esto hasta llegar al tablado, donde se apea:

¡Quién como ella,
la Serrana de la Vera!

Copla.

A dar flores sale al prado
la Serrana de la Vera,
bizarra puesta a caballo,
la Serrana de la Vera.
En crenchas lleva el tocado
la Serrana de la Vera,
ojos hermosos rasgados,
la Serrana de la Vera,
lisa frente, rojos labios,
la Serrana de la Vera,
pelo de ámbar, blancas manos,
la Serrana de la Vera,
cuerpo genzor y adamado,
la Serrana de la Vera.
¡Quién como ella,
la Serrana de la Vera!

2.º

A dar flores sale a valle
la Serrana de la Vera,
genzor cuerpo, hermoso talle,
la Serrana de la Vera.
Su belleza y su donaire,
la Serrana de la Vera,
viene enamorando el aire
la Serrana de la Vera.
Sus ojos negros y graves,
la Serrana de la Vera,
no hay quien mire que no adame

on horseback, comes GILA, La Serrana de la Vera, dressed in serrana or mountain style. The upper part of her dress has many devotional images.[17] *Her hair is loose, and she wears a feathered cap. She has a mountain knife, silvery buskins, and, under the saddle-cover, a rifle. The villagers sing the following before reaching the stage, where the Serrana dismounts.*

ENSEMBLE Is there anyone like her?
La Serrana de La Vera!

With flowers from the meadow.
La Serrana de La Vera!
On horseback, she's thrilling.
La Serrana de La Vera!
Hair parted down the middle.
La Serrana de La Vera!
Eyes lush and wide-open.
La Serrana de La Vera!
Ruby lips, shining forehead.
La Serrana de La Vera!
White hands, hair of amber.
La Serrana de La Vera!
What a beautiful body.
La Serrana de La Vera!

Is there anyone like her?
La Serrana de La Vera!

With flowers from the valley.
La Serrana de La Vera!
What a beckoning body.
La Serrana de La Vera!
Such bewitchment and beauty.
La Serrana de La Vera!
The breeze rushing behind her.
La Serrana de La Vera!
Her deep black eyes gazing.
La Serrana de La Vera!
She entraps in amazement.

la Serrana de la Vera.
Dios mil años mos la guarde
la Serrana de la Vera,
y la dé un galán amante,
la Serrana de la Vera,
para que con ella case,
la Serrana de la Vera,
y para a los Doce Pares,
la Serrana de la Vera.
¡Quién como ella,
la Serrana de la Vera!

(GILA apéase, y dice, tomando la escopeta de la silla del caballo:)

GILA — Lleva, Mingo, ese caballo
al pesebre, y del arzón
esa caza quite Antón.
CAPITÁN — (*Ap.:* ¡De puro admirado callo!
¡No he visto en hombre jamás
tan varonil bizarría!)
GIRALDO — Vengas con bien, hija mia.
GILA — ¡Oh, padre!
GIRALDO — ¡Gallarda estás!
Cada vez que te contemplo,
vida pienso que me añades,
Jordán de mi edad. ¡Que edades
sin fin vivas para ejemplo
de mujeres españolas!
A los jazmines, contigo,
¿cómo les fue, y entre el trigo,
a las rojas amapolas?
Los azules alhelíes,
¿han querido competir
con tus venas de zafir?
¿A tus labios carmesíes
atrevióse algún clavel?
¿Hubo algunas maravillas,
al nácar de tus mejillas,
descorteses?

La Serrana de La Vera!
May God keep her forever.
La Serrana de La Vera!
And grant her a lover.
La Serrana de La Vera!
To whom she'll be married.
La Serrana de La Vera!
In immortal pairing.
La Serrana de La Vera!

Is there anyone like her?
La Serrana de La Vera!

(Gila dismounts, taking the rifle from under the horse's saddle. She speaks.)

GILA Mingo, go stable this horse.
Antón, take off this saddle.
CAPTAIN (aside) I am speechless. Such an
Impressive show of manliness –
I have never seen such a thing,
Not even in a man.
GIRALDO Daughter,
You've made it back safely.
GILA Father!
GIRALDO You're looking splendid today.
You are my river of Jordan:
Every time I gaze at you,
Years are added to my life.
May you live forever – yes,
May you be an enduring
Example to Spanish women!
How did it go today among
The jasmine flowers, the flowing wheat,
And the meadows of scarlet poppies?
Did the violets wish to compete
With your gorgeous sapphire veins?
Did some carnation dare compare
To your shining crimson lips?
And were the common marigolds
Discourteous to the golden glow
Of your glorious cheeks?

GILA Un crüel
jabalí se me atrevió
solamente, mas de suerte,
que solicitó su muerte
por donde menos pensó.
GIRALDO ¿De qué modo?
GILA Yo corría
tras de un corzo al viento igual
y al descubrir el cristal
de una hermosa huente fría,
que hendo a unos ruiseñores
cariño, porque callaba,
y tan en tanto ensartaba
perlas en hilos de flores,
en colchones de alhelíes
un sangriento jabalí
vi echado, que desde allí
perlas trocaba a rubíes,
que tan caro le convida
la hermosa fuente de beberlas,
que por la sed de las perlas
daba la sangre y la vida.
Apenas sintió el roído
cuando, puesto en cuatro pies,
el fiero animal montés,
de espuma y sangre teñido,
desenvainó del cristal
de la huente los colmillos
que son mortales cochillos,
y el espumoso animal
al caballo arremetió,
terrible y determinado,
lo que alcanzó por un lado,
y hurtéle la vuelta yo.
Vuelve otra vez sobre mí,
y yo revuelvo sobre él,
y más airado y crüel,
el cerdoso jabalí

GILA The only thing discourteous
To me was a wild boar.
Fortunately it found its death
Where it least expected it.

GIRALDO How?

GILA Chasing a deer at the speed of the wind,
I reached the crystalline waters of
A cold and beautiful spring,
Its gentle murmur caressing the ear
Like the song of nightingales,
Its silvery surface a series of
Watery pearls threaded with flowers.
There I saw, on a bed of violets,
A blood-soaked wild boar.
Transforming pearls to rubies.
That lovely spring sweetly summoned
The thirsty beast to imbibe.
Lusty for those luscious jewels, he
Slowly surrendered his lifeblood.
The ferocious mountain beast
Had barely heard us approach when
He sprang up, stretched out his limbs, and
Drenched in foam and dyed in blood,
Unsheathed from the crystal waters
A pair of mortal daggers: his fangs.
The frothy creature launched himself
At my horse's exposed flanks
With sudden and terrifying force.
He managed to grab one flank,
I turned the horse in an instant,
Got the upper hand on the beast,
Then he got the upper hand on me,
Then I on him, then he on me,
Whirling and whirling around,
Until that cruel, arrogant swine

otra vez arremetió
a los pechos del caballo.
Pudo herillo, a no apartallo
con tanta destreza yo.
Vuelvo las ancas, aflojo
el freno, doyle al ijar
la espuela, y vuélveme a dar
asalto, en su sangre, rojo.
Tuerzo el cuerpo, y sobre el lado
izquierdo pongo el cañón,
corre el gatillo al fogón
y al pardo plomo colado
el sediento pedernal,
y apenas sufre que ocupe
la pólvora, cuando escupe
contra el sangriento animal
un rayo que le reciba
por la vista y las orejas,
y partiéndole las cejas
di con él patas arriba.
Maté este lobo después,
y ese oso fiero, señor,
y de la caza menor
alguna que entre los pies
el caballo atropellaba
y con los perros corrimos.
Y con esto nos volvimos,
como ardiendo el sol bajaba,
deseosa que esta tarde
vamos a ver a Plasencia
las fiestas, con tu licencia.

GIRALDO Muchos años Dios te guarde,
que yo, Gila, determino
acompañarte también.

GILA ¿Quién es este hombre de bien
que, tan galán, de camino,
estaba con vos aquí?

GIRALDO Es un Capitán

Dove into my horse's breast,
And if not for my tremendous skill,
Would have killed him there and then.
[I pried him off, turned his haunches,
Loosened the reins, then gave the horse
A vicious kick with my spurs.
The boar, bloody red, counter-attacked.][18]
I turned my body, propped myself up
On my left side, cocked my rifle –
Boom! The trigger faithfully
Delivered its fateful message.
Thirsty flirt gulped heavy lead,
In an instant the barrel spat
A bolt of blazing lightning, straight into
His eyes, parting his brow in two.
When I approached my feral foe
A moment later, all four legs were
Sticking straight up in the air,
And so I claimed my prize.
Later, I killed this wolf and bear.
We also got some lesser prey,
Trampled by our horses or
Run down by our trusty hounds.
With these prizes, we've returned,
As the blazing sun descends.
We hope to go to Plasencia
This evening, for the fiesta,
If you give us permission.

GIRALDO May God keep you always, Gila.
I mean to go with you as well.

GILA Who was that impressive man,
In travelling clothes, I saw you with? [19]

GIRALDO He's a captain.

GILA ¿Querrá
alojarse?
GIRALDO Claro está.
GILA Pues yo no quiero.
CAPITÁN Yo sí.
GILA ¿No hay más que quererlo vos?
CAPITÁN Aquí no pienso que hay más.
GILA No vi capitán jamás
tan resuelto, ¡vive Dios!
CAPITÁN Ni yo mujer que tan bien
lo jure.
GILA Si imagináis
que lo soy, os engañáis,
que soy muy hombre.
CAPITÁN Pues bien.
¿Qué importa, señora Gila,
cuando fuera su merced
dos Hércules?
GILA Pretended,
pues el hablar aniquila
a los que de hombres se precian,
que acortemos de razones,
que tales conversaciones
más que estiman menosprecian,
como dice el refrán,
y busque otro alojamiento
el Alférez o el Sargento
para el señor Capitán,
porque mi padre no aloja
sino es a mí solamente,
a su ganado, a su gente
y al güesped que se le antoja,
y a soldados, camarada,
aunque el Rey se lo soprique
nunca lo acostumbra. Pique,
que más abajo hay posada,
que en esta casa yo fío
que os la den de mala gana.

GILA Does he want lodging?
GIRALDO That's for certain.
GILA I don't want that.
CAPTAIN Well, I do.
GILA Is everything
A matter of what you want?
CAPTAIN That's all there is to it.
GILA Goddamit,
I've never seen someone so stubborn
Who goes by the name of Captain.
CAPTAIN I've never heard someone so foul-mouthed
Who goes by the name of woman.
GILA If you think that I'm a woman,
You're very much deceived:
I am very much a man.
CAPTAIN If you were Hercules ten times over
It wouldn't make a difference.
GILA Say what you want: words don't make a man.
But why waste time in debate?
Arguing diminishes us
Rather than making us great,
Or so the old saying goes.
So go call upon your sergeant
Or lieutenant to find
A lodging place for their Captain.
My father puts up only his daughter,
His livestock, his people, his chosen guests.
And as for soldiers, who cares
What the King himself requests.
Go. There's an inn right down the road.
No one wants you here.

CAPITÁN ¡Oh, qué cansada villana!
GILA ¡Oh, qué fanfarrón jodío!
CAPITÁN ¡Vive Dios, que hemos de ver
cómo me contradecís
alojarme!
GILA Vos venís
donde no queréis volver.
CAPITÁN ¡Ah, señor Alférez! ¡Hola,
señor Sargento!
GILA Esperad.
No os enojéis, y escuchad
aquesta palabra sola.
CAPITÁN ¿Qué quieres?
GILA Que os alojéis
muy en buen hora, que llanos
estamos ya.
CAPITÁN Al fin, villanos,
que nada por bien hacéis,
temiendo que la jineta
no hiciera el alojamiento,
¿cuál ha de ser mi aposento?
GILA ¡El cañón de esta escopeta!
CAPITÁN ¿Qué dices?
GILA ¡Procura entrar,
fanfarrón!
CAPITÁN ¡Escucha, advierte…
GILA ¡Vive Dios, que de esta suerte
os he de echar del lugar!

Éntrase el CAPITÁN, retirando, y GILA, poniéndole la escopeta a la vista, que lo hará muy bien la SEÑORA JUSEPA.

GIRALDO ¡Eso sí, y no quiera
sopetearnos nenguno!
PASCUAL. ¡Si hueran diez, como es uno,
lo propio, Giraldo, huera!
MINGO ¡Ojo, cuál va por la calle
el fanfarrón capitán!
VICENTE. ¡Mala Pascua y mal San Juan

CAPTAIN — You peasant bitch.
GILA — You arrogant Jew-blooded bastard.[20]
CAPTAIN — By God – if you dare turn me away.
GILA — You're crossing a line, Captain.
CAPTAIN — Sergeant! Lieutenant! Hallo!
GILA — Wait, no need to get upset.
I have one more word for you.
CAPTAIN — What do you want?
GILA — I want to wish you well
In finding a place a stay.
I'm glad we're parting on good terms.
CAPTAIN — You've done yourselves no favors, peasants.
Take a good look at the tip of my spear.
Where I am going to sleep tonight?
GILA — Staring straight into the barrel
Of this gun.
CAPTAIN — What are you saying?
GILA — Go ahead, try to enter this house,
You arrogant son of a bitch.
CAPTAIN — Listen to me.
GILA — By God above,
I'll run you straight out of town.

Exit the Captain, retreating, followed by Gila, who keeps the rifle in full sight, which the señora Jusepa should be able to do very well.

GIRALDO — That's right! No one treats us this way!
PASCUAL — If there were ten of him, she'd do the same!
MINGO — Look at that arrogant little Captain,
Running away!
VICENTE — Damn him on Easter!

le dé Dios, y nunca halle
en toda la Vera apenas
un soldado que le siga!

LLORENTE ¡Todo el Cielo le maldiga!

MINGO ¡Pardiobre, que me dan venas
de atordille desde aquí,
Giraldo, con un guijarro!

BRAS ¡Y si cojo de un chaparro
una estaca yo!

GIRALDO ¡Vení,
y no perdamos a Gila
de vista!

MINGO ¡Giraldo, vamos,
aunque si mal no miramos
los mocos le despabila,
y no hay de ella temer
con un hombre tan roín!

GIRALDO ¡Hija de Giraldo, al fin!
¡Volvé a cantar y tañer!

Éntranse cantando.

¡Quíen como ella,
la Serrana de la Vera!

Entre agora el CAPITÁN retirándose, y GILA, con la escopeta en los ojos, y dice él:

CAPITÁN Serrana hermosa y crüel,
¿dónde me intentas llevar?

GILA Esta es la cruz del lugar,
la horca aquélla, y aquel,
el camino de Plasencia,
aquel el de Jarandilla.
No volváis más a la villa
a tentarme de paciencia,
que os volaré, ¡vive Dios!,
mucho mejor que lo digo.
Basta lo que vos conmigo
y yo he pasado con vos

And damn him on Saint John's day!
And may he never recruit a soldier
Anywhere in all La Vera!

LLORENTE May heaven rain curses on him!

MINGO I'll smash his head with a cobblestone!

BRAS I'll make that scrub oak his stake!

GIRALDO Come on. Let's not let Gila
Out of our sight.

MINGO All right.
But unless we're greatly mistaken,
She'll clean the snot right out of his nose.
She has nothing to fear from
That pathetic little man.

GIRALDO She is my daughter, after all!
Strike up the music! Sing that song!

ENSEMBLE Is there anyone like her?
La Serrana de La Vera…!

They exit singing.

[Act One, Scene 2. The outskirts of Garganta la Olla.]

The Captain enters, retreating, followed by Gila, who is pointing the rifle at him. He says:

CAPTAIN Where do you intend to take me,
Cruel and beautiful Serrana?

GILA Here's the town cross. There's the gallows.
That's the road to Plasencia.
And over there, to Xarandilla.[21]
Don't try my patience by ever
Setting foot in this town again,
Or I'll set you flying, by God,
In a way I can't give words to.
What happened between us today

para que no segundéis,
que sufro mal demasías,
que a otras cuatro compañías
lo mismo hiciera que veis,
cuanto y más a un capitán
tan descortés y hablador.
Y adviértoos, que este rigor
pasará, a ser vos Roldán,
adelante si volvéis,
no solamente a mi casa,
sino al lugar, pues que pasa
lo que a vuestros ojos veis.
Y poneos a escoger
cuál de los caminos dos
más os agrada, y adiós. *Vase.*

CAPITÁN ¿Hay más notable mujer?
Haciéndome cruces quedo,
porque vence con valor,
con hermosura y amor,
y dos veces decir puedo
que vencido me ha dejado.
Hasta el campo me sacó,
que más rigor no se osó
con un recién azotado
que le apean del jumento
para desterralle. ¡Estoy
sin mí!

DON GARCÍA, alférez.

DON GARCÍA En vuestra busca voy,
y lo mismo hace el sargento.
¿Qué es lo que os ha sucedido,
señor Capitán?

CAPITÁN No sé,
que una mujer sola…

DON GARCÍA ¿Fue
la Serrana?

Must never happen again.
I'm not patient: what I'd do to you
I'd do to four whole companies,
And Roland himself if I had to.[22]
But you're just a sweet-talking Captain,
One man with no manners. Beware.
Come back to my house or town,
And you'll absorb the holy wrath
Of what's pointed at your eyes.
You've got two choices. Goodbye.

She exits.

CAPTAIN What an extraordinary woman!
I'm crossing myself in wonder.
She conquers with her courage first,
And then with her beauty and love,
And so she's conquered me, twice over.
She took me out to the countryside
And dared be more severe with me
Than with a penitent who's been
Whipped and flayed and stripped off his donkey
And sent into lonely exile.[23]
I am out of my mind.

Enter Don García, lieutenant.

DON GARCÍA I've been looking
All over for you, the Sergeant too.
What's happened to you, Captain?
CAPTAIN I don't know. One single woman…
DON GARCÍA La Serrana?

CAPITÁN ¡No ha tenido
Aquiles mayor valor,
aunque mis locos antojos
más temieron a sus ojos!
DON GARCÍA Si es la Serrana, señor
don Lucas, tiene en la Vera
notable fama de hermosa
y de mujer valerosa.
CAPITÁN Haced sacar la bandera
de la villa, don García,
que mejor será en Plasencia
levantalla, y con violencia
de toda una compañía
abrasar este lugar
y gozar esta mujer
tan brava.
DON GARCÍA Es buen parecer.
Bien podrás luego marchar,
que esta es belicosa gente,
y estando sin compañía
hará una superchería.
CAPITÁN Esta serrana valiente
he de rendir si me cuesta
mil vidas, Alférez.
DON GARCÍA Luego
puedes.
CAPITÁN De furia estoy ciego,
pero no es ocasión esta.
DON GARCÍA Determínate, que yo
solo a Garganta la Olla
abrasaré, y esa polla
que entre los gallos crïó
se la daré sazonada
en el plato que quisieres,
y todas cuantas mujeres
tiene dentro, si te agrada.
Resuélvete tú, y verás
el valor de don García.

CAPTAIN Not even Achilles
Had more courage than that woman.
Her eyes sparked fearful desires.
DON GARCÍA If you're speaking of La Serrana,
señor Don Lucas, she's famed
Throughout all of La Vera
For her boldness and beauty.
CAPTAIN Let's take down our flag, Don García.
Better to hoist it in Plasencia.
We can always come back with
A whole company of men
And burn this place to the ground
And enjoy that wild woman.
DON GARCÍA Good idea, our marching off.
These are belligerent people,
And without a company around,
They're bound to get unruly.[24]
CAPTAIN That courageous Serrana
Will submit to me, Lieutenant,
If it costs me a thousand men.
DON GARCÍA You could make her submit right now.
CAPTAIN I'm blind with rage, but the moment's not right.
DON GARCÍA Show some resolve. Some fight!
I could burn Garganta la Olla
To the ground all by myself,
And as for that chick raised like a cock,
I'll serve her up to you, well-seasoned.
Same goes for every woman in town.
Make up your mind! Be bold!
Let loose Don García!

CAPITÁN ¿No basta ser sangre mía
para intentar esto y más?
DON GARCÍA No hay sino decir. Yo quiero,
y remitillo a esta espada,
que el mundo en gustando es nada,
por la fe de caballero.

(Suenan relinchos de labradores.)

CAPITÁN Gente de la villa sale
que deben de ir a Plasencia
a las fiestas.
DON GARCÍA Tu paciencia
de salvaguardia les vale,
que por la fe de soldado
que habían de ver quién soy.
CAPITÁN Por ser capitán estoy
a esto, Alférez, obligado,
que, siendo oficial del Rey,
no es justa razón causar
alboroto en un lugar.
Mas yo romperé esta ley
en más cómoda ocasión,
si no mudan pareceres.
DON GARCÍA Míraslo como quien eres,
y obedecerte es razón.
Voy a sacar la bandera.
CAPITÁN Sáquese, y vamos de aquí.
(*Ap.:* ¡Loco me lleva, y sin mí,
la Serrana de la Vera!) *Vanse.*

Salgan DOS de la ciudad, en Plasencia.

1.º ¿Cuántos son los toros?
2.º Creo
que son doce, pero son
cada cual como un león.
1.º ¡Qué de ellos rodando veo,
si hay lanzadas y rejones,
y no lo saben hacer!

CAPTAIN	Isn't my own blood good enough To do all that and more?
DON GARCÍA	Just give the word, I'm ready. Put your faith in this brave sword – I swear to you as a gentleman, I want the world to have a taste!

(The whinnying of the farmers' horses is heard.)

CAPTAIN	The townspeople are leaving. They must be on their way to the Fiesta in Plasencia.
DON GARCÍA	Your patience is their safe conduct. I swear to you as a soldier – Let them see what I'm made of!
CAPTAIN	This is my obligation As Captain and King's officer, I have no right, Lieutenant, to Provoke a riot in this village, But I will gladly break the law On a more fitting occasion If they don't see things my way.
DON GARCÍA	You see things as the man you are, And I have no choice but obey. I'll go and lower the flag.
CAPTAIN	Lower it, and let's be gone. (aside) The Serrana de la Vera Is driving me out of my mind.

They exit.

[Act One, Scene 3. Plasencia.]

Enter two city people, in Plasencia.

1ST PERSON	How many bulls will there be?
2ND PERSON	Twelve, I think. Every last one a lion.
1ST	Look at the bullfighters closing in, Trying to land a good thrust of the lance.

2.º Sacres por fuerza ha de haber,
siendo los toros leones,
que volarán de las sillas,
más que hacia arriba, hacia abajo.
1.º Ese es notable trabajo,
aun haciendo el asta astillas.
2.º A los que ven desde lejos
fácil les parece todo,
y en el coso, de otro modo.
1.º Siempre seguí los consejos
de los que dicen que cosa
sin quien se puede pasar,
o hacella bien o mirar.
2.º La plaza está milagrosa.
1.º No la he visto así jamás.
2.º Bien te admiras y la estrañas.
1.º ¿Cómo es el juego de cañas?
2.º Capas y gorras no más,
porque lugar no tuvieron
para libreas, por ser
con tanta prisa el querer
pasar Sus Altezas.
1.º ¿Fueron
ciertas las nuevas de Alhama?
2.º Don Rodrigo Girón es
el que la puso a sus pies,
digna hazaña de su fama.
1.º Con justa causa le alaba
la castellana nación.
2.º Al fin Pacheco y Girón,
maestre de Calatrava.
1.º Él podrá poco, o pondrá
a sus pies del mismo modo
a Granada.
2.º El coso todo
de gente cubierto está,
y ocupando las ventanas
damas bizarras y bellas.

They can't find a good way in!
2ND If the bulls are roaring lions,
These men are soaring falcons,
About to go flying from their saddles.
1ST It's hard work, especially when
Your spear is shredded to splinters.
2ND Everything seems easily done
When you're watching from afar,
But when you're standing in the ring –
Well, that's another matter.[25]
1ST As the old saying goes: stand up and do it,
Or sit back, watch – and shut up.
2ND The plaza is amazing today.[26]
1ST I've never seen it this way before.
2ND It fills you with awe and longing.
1ST How will they do the joust with the darts?[27]
2ND In their standard cloaks and hats.
There's no time to change into
Full tournament attire because
Their Majesties will be here soon.
1ST Is it true, the news from Alhama?[28]
2ND Rodrigo Girón has the town
At his feet, an exploit worthy
Of his glorious family name.
1ST No wonder our Castilian nation
Rises up in praise of him.
2ND He's a Pacheco and Girón,
And Master of the Holy Order
Of the militia of Calatrava.[29]
1ST All he needs is to lift a finger
And he'll soon have all Granada
Stretched out at his feet.
2ND The plaza's filled!
Lovely women stare from every window.

1.º Hoy sale el sol con estrellas.
2.º Bellas son las plasencianas.
1.º ¿No tomaremos lugar
en un tablado?
2.º Tomemos,
porque después no podremos
sitio tan a gusto hallar.
1.º ¿Hacia qué acera os inclina
la voluntad?
2.º A esta acera.

(De adentro, vendiendo, diferentes voces.)

3.º ¡Limas dulces de la Vera!
4.º ¡Turrón!
5.º ¡Confitura fina!
6.º ¡Lindas camuesas y peros!
7.º ¡Cerezas!
8.º ¡Piñón mondado!
9.º ¡Azúcar blanco rosado!
AGUADOR ¡Agua y anís, caballeros!

UN MAESTRO DE ESGRIMA y UN MUCHACHO, con espadas y cascos.

MAESTRO Planta, Perico, el arnés
en este sitio.
PERICO Hoy es día
de poleo y valentía.

DOS BRAVOS, el UNO con espada, y el OTRO, que es ANDRÉS, vestido como carretero, sin ella, y con montera y polainas, y un capote de dos haldas, y debajo de él un coleto, y caída por detrás la capa.

GERÓNIMO ¿No hugaremos, Andrés?
ANDRÉS Gerónimo, en viendo entrar
de Garganta la Olla hente
tomaré la espada.
GERÓNIMO A veinte
de Cuacos en su lugar
dieron mucha pesadumbre
las fiestas pasadas.

1ST The sun is shining, and the stars.
2ND They're pretty, these Plasencians.
1ST Should we find a place in the grandstand?
2ND Yes, while there's still space left.
1ST Which way do we go?
2ND This way.

(They exit.)
(Offstage, various voices, selling things.)

3RD PERSON Candied limes!
4TH PERSON Almond paste!
5TH PERSON Sweets!
6TH PERSON Fresh apples and pears!
7TH PERSON Cherries!
8TH PERSON Pine nuts!
9TH PERSON Pink and white sugar crystals!
WATER SELLER Licorice water, my friends!

Enter a Fencing Master and a young man with swords and helmets.[30]

MASTER Set the equipment here, Perico.
PERICO Today's a day for bragging rights.

Enter two roughnecks. One, Gerónimo, has a sword. The other, Andrés, dressed like a cart driver, does not have a sword. He wears a cloth hunting cap, rural-style gaiters, a small cape or cloak with a fur doublet underneath, and has an over-cloak thrown over his shoulder.[31]

GERÓNIMO Ready to stir things up, Andrés?
ANDRÉS Gerónimo, the moment
I lay eyes on anyone
From Garganta la Olla,
My hand goes straight to that sword.
GERÓNIMO Remember last fiesta time?
They gave twenty men from Cuacos
A lot of trouble.[32]

ANDRÉS Hoy,
esperándolos estoy.
GERÓNIMO Siempre tienen de costumbre
bravear en su lugar,
aunque los de esa aldegüela
les mearon la pajuela.
MAESTRO ¡Ea, galanes, entrar
para hacer nombre de Dios!
GERÓNIMO ¿Qué responde Andrés a eso?
ANDRÉS Pues lo dice el so Maeso,
huguemos ambos a dos.
GERÓNIMO Tenga, mancebo, esta capa
y esta espada.
ANDRÉS Tengamé
esta mía.
MAESTRO Jueguesé.

(Toman las espadas, y dice:)

ANDRÉS No he de perdonar al Papa,
no siendo de mi lugar.
MAESTRO Sea para bien la estrena.
Toquen casco.

(Tocan casco, y luego como acostumbran sus idas y venidas.)

ANDRÉS Dorabuena.
MAESTRO Limpio, y solo señalar,
que aquí a enseñar se camina,
y es lo demás borrachera.

(Entretanto que desde adentro se pregona:)

3.° ¡Limas dulces de le Vera!
4.° ¡Turrón!
5.° ¡Confitura fina!
6.° ¡Lindas camuesas y peros!
7.° ¡Cerezas!
8.° ¡Piñón mondado!
9.° ¡Azúcar blanco rosado!
AGUADOR ¡Agua y anís, caballeros!

ANDRÉS — Not today.
I'm here, ready, waiting for them.
GERÓNIMO — They talk tough when they're at home.
We'll give them a whiff of their village
When they're gagging on a piss-soaked stick.
MASTER — Come on, brave lads. Let's get started!
GERÓNIMO — What does Andrés say to that?
ANDRÉS — Like Master says: let's get started.
GERÓNIMO — Take this sword and cloak, my friend.[33]
ANDRÉS — This one's mine.
MASTER — Prepare to face off.

(They take their swords, and Andrés says:)

ANDRÉS — I'd attack the Pope himself:
The Pontiff's not from my hometown.
MASTER — Looking good, lads. Touch helmets.

(They touch helmets.)

ANDRÉS — Ready, set.
MASTER — Fight cleanly – go!

(They start the usual fencing passes.)

MASTER — Remember, it's a demonstration.
Our purpose here is pure instruction.
Save the drunken scuffling for later.

(Meanwhile those offstage bark out:)

3RD PERSON — Candied limes!
4TH PERSON — Almond paste!
[5TH PERSON — Sweets!
6TH PERSON — Fresh apples and pears!
7TH PERSON — Cherries!
8TH PERSON — Pine nuts!
9TH PERSON — Pink and white sugar crystals!
WATER SELLER — Licorice water, my friends!

MAESTRO ¡Yo la vi! Vaya otro, y tiento
con la vista.
GERÓNIMO Eso buscamos.

GIRALDO agora, y MINGO, con capa, puesto a lo gracioso, de bravo, y MADALENA y GILA, con rebozos en la cara, de volante, y sombreros de palma, y ferreruelos.

GILA ¡A lindo tiempo llegamos!
MADALENA Camínase por el viento,
Gila, cuando a fiestas es.
GILA Estas, prima Madalena,
son de mayor gusto.
MADALENA ¿Llena
la plaza de hombres no ves?
GILA Como los Reyes honrar
esta ciudad han querido,
toda la Vera ha venido,
que no ha faltado lugar.
Rabiando vengo por ver
a la Reina, porque de ella,
después de decir que es bella,
dicen que es brava mujer,
que, al lado de su marido,
–que le guarde Dios mil años–,
la ven her hechos estraños,
mas tal madre la ha parido
y tal padre la engendró.
MADALENA Su valor pintado han
en el Príncipe don Juan.
GILA Madalena, en viendo yo
mujeres de esta manera
me vuelvo de gusto loca.
MAESTRO Esta vaya, y punto en boca.

De adentro.

3.° ¡Limas dulces de la Vera!
GIRALDO Gila, tomemos lugar.
MINGO Siempre que en el coso estoy,

MASTER That's a touch! Another round.
Remember, just the slightest touch.
GERÓNIMO That's exactly what we're here for.][34]

Enter Giraldo; Mingo, with his cloak like a comic tough-guy; and Madalena and Gila, their faces covered by their head-dresses, with palm-leaf hats and simple collarless cloaks.

GILA We've come at the perfect moment.
MADALENA Whenever there's a fiesta,
Gila, you rush there like the wind.
GILA This one's the best, Madalena.
MADALENA Look at the plaza, filled with men.
GILA [All La Vera has turned out to
See our noble monarchs who
Come to honor this city, cousin.][35]
I'm longing to see the Queen.
[They say she's not just beautiful
But brave and tough, and with her husband –
May God protect him forever! –
She's achieved remarkable things.
But after all, she's daughter to
Quite a mother and father.[36]
MADALENA You see their likeness in her son,
Don Juan, Prince of Asturias.[37]
GILA Madalena, women like that
Drive me crazy with pleasure.
MASTER Again. Let's have some quiet.[38]

Offstage:

THIRD PERSON Candied limes!][39]
GIRALDO Let's find a grandstand.
MINGO Whenever I'm close to the bull ring,

de mí imagino que doy
un olor particular,
que debe de ser de miedo,
y es para el que tengo al lado…

De adentro.

9.° ¡Azúcar blanco rosado!
MINGO ¡Y membrillo de Toledo!
GILA Juego de armas hay aquí.
Lleguemos, padre, a mirar,
que no faltará lugar.
GIRALDO ¡Tal inclinación no vi!
MADALENA Erró la naturaleza,
Gila, en no herte varón.
GILA ¡Ay, prima, tienes razón!

De adentro.

8.° ¡Piñon mondado!
7.° ¡Cereza!
ANDRÉS Llegando van forasteros.
Sienta, Gerónimo.
GERÓNIMO Andrés,
sí haré para entrar dempués.

De adentro.

AGUADOR ¡Agua y anís, caballeros!

(Toma GERÓNIMO su capa y su espada, y echa un cuarto en el casco que se quita el MUCHACHO de la cabeza. Toma el montante el MAESO y hace plaza agora.)

MAESTRO ¡Plaza, hidalgos! ¡Fuera, fuera!
¡Guardar los pies!
GILA Mingo, toma
la espada tú.
MINGO ¿Yo? ¡Mahoma,
con este! ¡De la montera,
Gila, la puede tomar!
GILA ¡Vive Dios, que eres gallina!

I seem to sense I'm emitting
A very particular odor,
Which is the smell of utter terror
Dripping down my backside for
The pleasure of my nearest neighbor.

Offstage:

9TH PERSON Pink and white sugar crystals!
MINGO And ripe quinces from Toledo,
Bursting with pulpy brown juice!
GILA There's a fencing match over here.
Come on, father, let's take a look.
We can find a place to watch later.
GIRALDO Have you seen anything like it?!
MADALENA Nature should have made you a man.
GILA Ah, cousin, you're right about that!

Offstage:

8TH PERSON Pine nuts!
7TH PERSON Cherries!
ANDRÉS Outsiders.
And they're coming this way.
Put down the sword, Gerónimo.
GERÓNIMO Only if I get my chance later.

Offstage:

[WATER SELLER] Licorice water, my friends!

(Gerónimo takes his cloak and sword and tosses a coin into the helmet which the young man has taken off. The Master takes a broadsword and gets the space ready.)

MASTER Give way, gentlemen! Stand back!
Watch your feet.
GILA Mingo, take the sword.
MINGO Me? Against that one in the cape?
Better Mohammed! Gila, take it.
GILA God help me, you're a chicken!

MINGO Pues si eso te da mohína,
yo te quiero contentar,
que quiero salir por ti
esta vez descalabrado.
GILA Entra tú determinado,
y ten hígados y di
que te descalabre.
MINGO Voy,
aunque con miedo crüel.
GILA Escucha, déjate de él
cargar la espada.
MINGO Ya estoy
en lo que dices.
GILA Y luego
alza y tírale un mandoble
que, aunque la espada se doble,
saque de los cascos huego,
y déjalo luego estar,
que aquí estoy yo.
MINGO Que no quiero
contra aqueste carretero
más, Gila, que verme entrar.
Mira del modo que tomo
la espada y cómo me quito
la capa.
ANDRÉS Ya estoy agito
de este payo.
MINGO Y mira cómo
voy entrando.
GILA Siempre tieso
y a la vista. Eso me agrada.
MINGO Un cuervo llevo en la espada.
Apártese, so Maeso.
MAESTRO ¡Toquen casco!
ANDRÉS ¡Dorabuena!
MAESTRO Limpio.
MINGO Yo tendré cuidado.
MADALENA Bravamente Mingo ha entrado.

MINGO Then let me make you happy:
For you and you alone, dear Gila,
I'll go and get my skull smashed in.
GILA Go ahead, with determination.
Show some guts – if they smash your skull,
So be it.
MINGO I'm going in, shaking with terror.
GILA Listen, let him take his sword…
MINGO I'm all ears
GILA Then lunge forward
And give him a good long slash,
And if your sword folds back on itself,
Use your helmet to spout flames
And put the fellow in his place.
I'm here for you.
MINGO I'd prefer not to.
What do I want with a cart driver?
Maybe just one quick parry.
Look, hey, I'm drawing my sword!
Hey, I'm taking off my cloak!
ANDRÉS I'm sick of this stupid bumpkin.
MINGO Now I'm making my first move!
GILA Keep it rigid. That's how I like it.
MINGO My sword's got claws like a crow.
Back off, Master!
MASTER Touch helmets.
ANDRÉS Get ready, get set.
MASTER Fight cleanly – go!
MINGO Believe me, it will be clean.
MADALENA Mingo's making a brave entrance.

GILA ¿Pues no ha de entrar, Madalena,
estando yo aquí?
GIRALDO Yo estoy
remozándome de ver
jugar las armas. Ayer
tal día como el que es hoy,
me parece que hue el día
que en este mismo lugar,
¡ah, mocedad!, a pesar
de la mayor valentía
que tuvo toda la Vera,
a un bravo di en qué entender.
Todo pasa por correr
tan breve la edad ligera.

(Agora vuelven a la segunda ida y venida. Dale en la cabeza, y suelta la espada.)

ANDRÉS Un pan le he de dar agora,
si puedo, como unas nueces.
MINGO Esto no es para dos veces.
Entre otro, amigo.
GILA ¡Enbuenhora!

(Arremeten GERÓNIMO y GILA a la espada, y cógela GILA.)

GERÓNIMO Tarde llegué y, ¡vive Dios,
que es mujer la que ha tomado
la espada!
GIRALDO Gila, ¿en qué has dado?
GILA Ya lo veréis, padre, vos.
Ten la capa, Madalena,
que a este bravo pienso her
que me sueñe.
ANDRÉS ¿Una mujer
toma la espada?
MINGO No suena
una calabaza más.
Algo pago por vacío
en los cascos.

GILA — And why shouldn't he, Madalena?
I'm right here to protect him.

GIRALDO — Seeing these young fellows fencing,
I'm tingling like a boy again.
It seems like only yesterday,
On this same spot, a day like today –
O daring days of my youth! –
I showed one of these tough guys
What's for, and did it before the eyes
Of La Vera's best and bravest.
Time is short, everything flies,
And life is light as a feather.

(They do a second set of passes. Andrés gives him Mingo a blow to the head, and Mingo drops his sword.)

ANDRÉS — That was just the basic loaf.
Now I stuff it with extra nuts.

MINGO — You won't get away with it twice!
Someone help me? Friend?

GILA — Here I am!

(Gerónimo and Gila both go for the sword, and Gila grabs it.)

GERÓNIMO — I got there late and, God help me,
A woman has grabbed the sword!

GIRALDO — Gila, what's gotten into you?

GILA — You'll see in a minute, father.
Take my cloak, Madalena,
I'm going to make this roughneck
See me in his dreams tonight.

ANDRÉS — A woman with a sword?!

MINGO — My head's rattling like a gourd,
My brain's ringing like a cow bell,
And my poor skull is swelling up
Like a pig's bladder.

ANDRÉS ¡Bravo brío!
MINGO Con carreteros, no más,
que es gran gente de Chinchón
y, ¡vive Dios!, que el que tiento,
que es otra cabeza, y siento
en el alma el coscorrón,
que imagino que también
ha quedado no sé cómo.
¡Oh, carretero de plomo,
mala pedrada te den,
derríbente las encías
con un almirez, un boj
te mate! ¡Para reloj
famosa mano tenías,
que asentara lindamente
cuando dieras el cahiz!
ANDRÉS Señora Aldonza, o Beatriz,
si es su amigo o su pariente
el payo del coscorrón
y le pretende vengar,
busque uno de su lugar
y llevará otro chichón,
que a mujeres tengo miedo,
sí, ¡por ell agua de Dios!,
y más si son como vos.
GILA Bien sé que dársele puedo,
mi señor, carro o carreta,
más que por mujer, por hombre.
ANDRÉS ¡Lindo dicho!
GILA No os asombre.
MINGO Plega a Dios que no se meta
Gila, por querer ser brava,
donde no pueda salir.
Bien nos pudiéramos ir,
que ya yo me contentaba
con que haya sido chichón
el tajo del carretero,
aunque hue Tajo y hue Duero.

ANDRÉS What spirit!
MINGO I'm done with these damned cart drivers.
Always walloping you with some
Heavy load, special delivery.
I seem to have grown a second head.
My whole body's one big bruise.
Even my soul is black and blue.
O cart driver, may someone soak you
In a shower of heavy lead,
Ring your noggin like a church bell,
Or smash your face with a boxwood tree,
To put it a little more bluntly.
You've got two hands, just like a clock
But they've struck me twelve times over.
ANDRÉS My sweet señora Aldonza –
Or should I call you Beatricé?[40] –
If this gallant country bumpkin
With the swollen pumpkin head
Is your friend or relation,
And you mean to avenge him,
Find a man to do your bidding,
Some fellow from your little village,
And I'll deliver another package.
By God, I'm scared of women! –
Especially ones who look like you.
GILA I could send you packing, señor,
Slow like a wagon, fast like a horse,
But more like a man than a woman.
ANDRÉS Well said.
GILA Then get ready.
MINGO I hope to God Gila doesn't
Try to show how tough she is by
Entering while there's still an exit.
We could quietly slink away
To tend to the fat package
The cart driver just delivered:
What I mean is, we could beat it
Before I get another beating.

GIRALDO No hay quien la meta en razón.
MAESTRO Doncella, siente la espada
y no nos entrampe el huego.
GILA Señor Maeso, yo huego,
y ya la tengo empuñada,
y no de her otra cosa
que la que digo.
MAESTRO Pues vaya.
GILA Mujer soy solo en la saya.
MAESTRO Y seréis mujer famosa.
ANDRÉS Al fin, señora doncella,
¿quiere hugar?
GILA Es antojo.
ANDRÉS ¡Por San Rorro, si me enojo,
que pueden doblar por ella!
GILA Jugar y callar parece
mucho mejor.
MAESTRO ¡Nunca vi
tal mujer!
GILA Yo siempre hui
de este parecer.
MAESTRO ¡Merece
corónica este valor!
¡Brava postura, famoso
partir cerrado y airoso!
¡No pudo hacerlo mejor
el mismo que lo ha inventado,
por vida de maese Juan!
Reconociéndose van.
GILA Este es revés por un lado.

(Cárgale la espada ANDRÉS, y ella le da muy bien, y mete el montante.)

MAESTRO Ya la vi. Basta.
ANDRÉS Y aun yo
la he sentido, y me ha aturdido,
¡vive Dios!
GILA Esto no ha sido
nada, ¡por Dios!, que corrió

GIRALDO Can she be brought to her senses?
MASTER Lay down your sword, fair maiden.
Please don't disturb our game.
GILA Master, I am joining in.
You see my hand gripping this sword?
I will do as I say.
MASTER All right.
GILA I am a woman in dress only.
MASTER You're a woman to remember.
ANDRÉS Ready, fair maiden?
GILA My pleasure.
ANDRÉS I swear on Saint Rory, holy patron of
Miserable, whining, bawling babies:
Bells are going to toll for you! [41]
GILA Why don't you just shut up and fight?
MASTER I've never seen such a woman!
GILA And I have always fled from
Being seen as a woman.
MASTER This amazing act of valor
Deserves recounting in some ballad.
Look at her impressive posture,
The unyielding way she advances –
The man who invented the art of fencing
Couldn't have done it better.
On the life of the great sword-maker,
The glorious Juan de la Horta[42] –
They are finally facing off!
GILA Watch me, backwards, forwards, sideways!

(Andrés charges at her with the sword, and she gives him a good blow, blocking him.)

MASTER That's a palpable touch – enough.
ANDRÉS It hit me, it stunned me, God help me.
GILA God help you, that was nothing.

la espada sobre la suya.
¡Vaya otra!

MAESTRO ¡Estraña mujer!

(Metiendo el montante.)

GILA So Maeso, esta ha de ser.
MAESTRO Aquí es bien que se concluya.
Siente, Andrés.
MINGO Pienso que siente
lo mismo que yo sentí.
MAESTRO ¡En toda mi vida vi
una mujer tan valiente!
ANDRÉS ¡Que esto hue buscar mohínas
con todo el lugar sospecho!
GERÓNIMO Digo que ha sido mal hecho.
GILA ¡Mienten como unas gallinas!

(Da sobre ellos GILA con la espada de esgrima, y GERÓNIMO desenvaina la suya, y ANDRÉS con la que tiene en la mano.)

MAESTRO ¡Asienta, mujer, la espada!
GILA ¡Ya es tarde!
MAESTRO ¡Derribaréte
con el montante!
GILA ¡Ea, vete!

(Dale al MAESTRO.)

MAESTRO ¿Al maestro cuchillada?
GILA Por esto se dijo.
MAESTRO ¡Espera!
GILA ¿Dónde, gallinas, me voy?
¡Ah, perros, hüid, que soy
la Serrana de la Vera!
GIRALDO ¡Hija, Gila!
GILA ¡Apartaos, padre!
¡No os pierda el respeto aquí!
GIRALDO ¡Pondré las manos en ti,
por el siglo de tu madre!

	Just a quick run of sword over sword.
	Come on. Again.
MASTER	Strange woman.

(The Master puts his broadsword between them.)

GILA	Master, this is meant to be.
MASTER	It's best to bring this to conclusion.
	Put the sword away, Andrés.
MINGO	I wish she put him away,
	The same way he put me away.
MASTER	I have never in my life
	Seen such a courageous woman.
ANDRÉS	I bet she has problems with
	Every last person she meets.
GERÓNIMO	I say this whole fight is fixed.
GILA	You lie like a pair of hens!

(Gila attacks them with the fencing sword and Gerónimo unsheathes his, while Andrés attacks with the one in his hand.)

MASTER	Put the sword away, woman!
GILA	Too late!
MASTER	I'll use my broadsword!
GILA	Go away!

(She attacks the Master.)

MASTER	Slashing at the Master?
GILA	So the saying goes.
MASTER	Wait!

[Exit Andrés and Gerónimo.]

GILA	I'll hunt you down, you clucking hens!
	Fine, you dogs! Go, run away!
	I am La Serrana de la Vera!
GIRALDO	Gila!
GILA	Get away from me,
	Father, or lose my respect.
GIRALDO	For the sake of your dear mother,
	I'll lay these two hands on you,

¡Quebraréte este bordón
en la cabeza!
MADALENA Giraldo,
pues no hay remedio, dejaldo.
MINGO ¡Voyme con mi coscorrón!
GILA ¡Ah, gallinas!
MADALENA El decoro,
enojada, ha de perderos.

Salga el que vende agua, y en diciendo este verso le quiebre el cántaro GILA, y digan de adentro:

AGUADOR ¡Agua y anís, caballeros!

De adentro.

¡Guarda el toro! ¡Guarda el toro!
MINGO ¡Aun esto huera peor!
Voy a subirme a un tablado.
GILA Como a toro me han dejado.
Conocieron mi furor.
Pésame que con espadas
y el montante se me fueron,
pero en efeto huyeron
como gallinas mojadas.
Tomaos eso que os lleváis,
pues para volver cuitados,
como dicen, trasquilados,
con la Serrana os tomáis,
con la que a brazo partido
mata al oso, al jabalí,
con la que un molino así
mil veces ha detenido,
con la que arroja más alta
la barra que el pensamiento,
con la que aventaja el viento
cuando corre o cuando salta,
con quien güesos y costillas
luchando a un hombre deshace,
con la que en las manos hace

I'll break this walking stick of mine
Over your stubborn head.
MADALENA Leave her,
Giraldo, there's no use.
MINGO Both my heads are bidding farewell.
GILA Chickens!
MADALENA Calm down, Gila,
You're losing your decorum.

Enter the licorice water vendor.

WATER SELLER Licorice water, my friends!

Gila smashes his pitcher, and those offstage say:

VOICES Watch for the bull! Watch for the bull!
MINGO And I thought it couldn't get worse.
I'm going up to the grandstand.

[Exit everyone but Gila.]

GILA They've left me alone with the bull.
They felt my wrath, then ran off,
Like a gaggle of wet hens,
Taking their swords with them.
Fine, take with you what you brought!
You came to shear yourselves some wool
And ended up getting shorn, you fools!
You picked a fight with La Serrana,
She who with her own bare hands
Slew the bear and wild boar,
She who stops the fearsome force
Of a mighty whirling windmill
And hurls the rustic javelin
To a place beyond the wind.
She who when she sprints and leaps
Outdistances the wind as well,
[And when she wrestles with a man,
Reduces him to a side of ribs,
A pair of soft-boiled eggs.
She who with a flash of her fist

tres herraduras astillas,
    con quien, como mimbres tiernos
corta una encina, una oliva,
con la que un toro derriba
asiéndole por los cuernos,
    con la que, en medio, el furor
detiene un carro de bueyes.

Tocan atabalillos, y salen arriba a una ventana DON FERNANDO y DOÑA ISABEL, y siéntanse en dos sillas.

Ya parece que los Reyes
salen a este corredor.
    ¡Más agradables presencias
en toda mi vida vi!
Helles quiero desde aquí
dos corteses reverencias.
    Guárdeos Dios, Reyes Cristianos,
y dempués que ambos viváis
cuatro mil años, os vais
al cielo dadas las manos,
    porque casados tan buenos,
como hiedra y olmo, es bien
que aquí y en el Cielo estén
jamás de gozarse ajenos.
    Que de vos, alta señora,
ha muchos días que estoy
enamorada, y os doy
los parabienes agora
    de los triunfos que gozáis
de las cosas que habéis hecho,
que bien el valor del pecho
en el semblante mostráis.
    Ruego a Dios que no paréis
hasta ganar a Granada,
porque dempués coronada
de sus granates quedéis,
    que dirán bien en la frente
de tan divina amazona.

Smashes horseshoes to tiny bits,
Who fells olive trees and sturdy oaks
As if they were the thinnest willows,
And stops oxen in their tracks.
Yes, she grabs the bull by the horns and,
Flipping it, rips it to pieces.][43]

Kettledrums sound, and enter from above, at a window, King Ferdinand and Queen Isabella. They sit down in a pair of chairs.

It looks like the King and Queen
Are making their royal entrance.
Never before have I ever seen
People of such pleasing presence.
I'll pay them my respects from here.
May God keep you, Christian monarchs!
May you reign four thousand years!
May you, at the end of that time,
Ascend to heaven, hand in hand,
For partnerships as fine as yours
Are like the ivy and the elm.
May you both enjoy each other's
Company on earth and heaven,
And may you never be apart.
[As for you, high and great lady,
For many days I have been
Hopelessly in love with you.
I offer you congratulations
For your triumphs and achievements:
The ample courage within your breast
Finds perfect reflection in
The perfection of your appearance.
May you conquer all Granada!
May you be crowned with blazing garnets!
How good they'll look good upon your brow,
Amazon goddess among us.

Vos tenéis gentil persona,
y mal haya yo si miente
en cuanto dice de vos
la fama, y que, si hombre fuera,
por vos sola me perdiera,
y aun así lo estoy, ¡por Dios!
Perdone, hermosa Isabel,
vuestro Fernando dichoso,
que lo hue en ser vueso esposo,
como vos en serlo de él.
Con esto, a Dios, que de mal
vos libre, y quede con vos,
y echadme entrambos a dos
vuesa bendición real,
que de hinojos os adoro.

FERNANDO ¡Qué serrana tan graciosa!

ISABEL ¡Y cuanto ser puede, hermosa!

(De adentro.)

¡Guarda el toro! ¡Guarda el toro!

FERNANDO Bizarro toro han sacado.

(Pónese en pie LA SERRANA.)

GILA Hoy he de her por serviros
una suerte, sin pediros
licencia, pues me ha encontrado
en el coso la ocasión,
y yo a Isabel enamoro.

De adentro.

¡Guarda el toro! ¡Guarda el toro!

Entren cayendo y levantándose ALGUNOS, y MINGO, caídas las bragas, y huyendo y diciendo:

MINGO ¡Aun este es peor chichón!
No temí en balde de estar,
pues esto pude temer,
en el coso sin saber
la trasera asegurar.

You have such a charming figure –
Strike me down if you don't live up to
Your exalted reputation!
Were I a man, I would lose myself
For you, in fact, I am lost
Already, lost, God help me.][44]
Pardon, beautiful Isabella,
But your honored Ferdinand
Is blessed to call himself your husband,
And you his wife, and so I say:
May God keep you free from harm!
And may you bestow your royal blessing.
I kneel here before you both
In awe and adulation.

FERDINAND What an amusing serrana!

ISABELLA And as beautiful a being
As there can possibly be.

(Offstage:)

[VOICES] Watch for the bull! Watch for the bull!

FERDINAND That's quite a bull they've let loose!

(The Serrana rises.)

GILA Today is a day I must serve you
Without asking for your license,
For I find myself in the ring,
In love with Queen Isabella.

Offstage:

[VOICES] Watch for the bull! Watch for the bull!

Enter some people falling over themselves, and Mingo with his breeches down, running away, saying:

MINGO This bruise is worse than the first.
I was fully justified
To be fully terrified.
Yes, when you're caught in the ring,
You need to cover your own ass.

GILA ¿Dónde vas como redina,
Mingo, todo desbragado?

Entre MINGO huyendo.

MINGO ¡Voy huyendo, que me ha echado
el toro una melecina!
GILA ¡Escupiendo espuma al cielo
viene el toro! Yo me arrojo,
que si los cuernos le cojo,
le he de her medir el suelo.

Éntrese arremetiendo hacia el vestuario.

ISABEL Loca aquella labradora,
Nuño, al parecer está.
DON NUÑO Por los cuernos asió ya
al toro feroz, y agora
le rinde como si fuera
una oveja.
FERNANDO ¡Qué osadía!

Descúbrese agora entre los paños la cabeza del toro solamente, y ella echándole patas arriba.

GILA Ya saben la huerza mía
los novillos de la Vera.
FERNANDO ¡Qué valerosa mujer!
ISABEL ¡No he visto mayor valor!
FERNANDO ¡Hola, don Nuño!
DON NUÑO ¡Señor!
FERNANDO Mercedes le quiero hacer
a esa mujer. Sabed de ella
de adónde es.
DON NUÑO ¡Ah, labradora!,
¿de adónde sois?
ISABEL Enamora
verla tan valiente y bella.
GILA Con reverencia y perdón,
soy de Garganta la Olla,
que de tan bizarra polla

GILA Where are you running, crazy devil?
By the way, your pants are down.
MINGO Doctor Bull has administered an
Enema. In case you didn't notice.

Exit Mingo, running away.

GILA Here comes the bull, spitting foam
To the heavens, spewing spittle.
I hurl myself into action:
If I can catch him by the horns,
I'll use him to measure dirt.

She exits, going into the dressing room.[45]

ISABELLA That village girl seems to be
Out of her mind, Don Nuño.
DON NUÑO She's grabbed that bull by the horns.[46]
Now the brute is surrendering
Like a lamb.
FERDINAND What audacity!

The head of the bull is revealed from behind the backdrop, while Gila throws it to the ground with its feet up.[47]

GILA Let that be a lesson to
Every young bull in La Vera.
FERDINAND What courage for a woman!
ISABELLA I have never seen greater.
FERDINAND Don Nuño!
DON NUÑO Señor?
FERDINAND I want to show
That woman my appreciation.
Find out where she's from.
DON NUÑO Hey!
Village girl! Where are you from?
ISABELLA Seeing such courage and beauty,
You fall in love.
GILA With due respect
I am from Garganta la Olla,
The offspring of a lovely chick

fue otra igual el cascarón
que no hue menos gentil.
DON NUÑO ¿Qué nombre tenéis?
ISABEL Llamalda.
GILA Llámanme Gila Giraldo,
hija de Giraldo Gil.
ISABEL La labradoraza es brava.

(Tocan cajas de adentro.)

FERNANDO ¿Estos qué atambores son?
DON NUÑO De don Rodrigo Girón,
maestre de Calatrava.
ISABEL El Maestre viene. Alguna
nueva nos trae, pues marchando
entra en Plasencia, Fernando.
DON NUÑO Ya el bravo Girón de Osuna
llega.
FERNANDO ¡Estraña novedad!
ISABEL Algo será de Granada.
GILA En el valor de su espada
muestra el traje y majestad.

Entre el MAESTRE DE CALATRAVA, DON RODRIGO, en cuerpo, de negro, con plumas negras en el sombrero, y una ropilla como vaquero cerrada por delante, y en medio del pecho, una cruz, mayor que las ordinarias de Calatrava, y bastón, y haciendo sus reverencias diga:

DON RODRIGO Católicos monarcas de Castilla,
Isabel y Fernando, a quien el Cielo
prospere, amén, y en la española orilla
os haga tributar el indio suelo,
entrando por el río de Sevilla,
que fue al valor de vuestro santo agüelo
espejo, de sus climas más remotas
todos los años dos bizarras flotas.
Yo llegué a Salamanca con la gente
castellana, estremeña y andaluza,
al orden que me distes obediente,
después de la postrera escaramuza,

	Who laid a no less lovely egg
	Out of which I proudly hatched.
ISABELLA	Call her over.
DON NUÑO	What's your name?
GILA	You can call me Gila Giraldo,
	Daughter to Giraldo Gil.
ISABELLA	That is one tough village girl.

(Drums sound from offstage.)

FERDINAND	Why are they beating those drums?
DON NUÑO	They're for Don Rodrigo Girón,
	Master of Calatrava.[48]
ISABELLA	He must bring news, marching so boldly
	Into the heart of Plasencia.
DON NUÑO	The great Girón de Osuna arrives!
FERDINAND	Absolutely remarkable.
ISABELLA	It must concern Granada.
GILA	The grandeur of his uniform
	Reveals the power of his sword.

Enter the Master of Calatrava, Don Rodrigo Girón, uncloaked, in black, with black feathers in his hat, with a rancher's apron tied in the front, and a larger-than-normal Calatrava cross on his chest, and a staff.[49] *He pays his respects, saying:*

DON RODRIGO	Illustrious monarchs who rule Castile,[50]
	Blesséd Ferdinand and Isabella,
	Whose Spanish shore is laid with golden tribute
	Paid by far-flung lands of distant Indies,
	Flowing up the swift Sevillian river,[51]
	Whose majestic waters brightly mirror
	The boundless courage of your holy ancestors
	As two magnificent gilded fleets per annum
	Gather from remote climes endless treasure.
	I come by way of nearby Salamanca,
	Accompanied by brave Castilian warriors,
	Andalusian as well, and Extremaduran,
	In strict obedience to your royal order,
	Having completed to fullest satisfaction

adonde cuerpo a cuerpo di al valiente
Abayaldos zegrí y al gomel Muza,
entre Ronda y Morón, muerte, a despecho
de un morisco escuadrón por mí deshecho.
Hallé llorando a todos vuestra ausencia,
pero en vuestro retrato generoso
vuestro mismo valor, vuestra prudencia
y vuestro mismo pecho valeroso
que las precisas causas que a Plasencia
os trujeron me dijo, y del forzoso
socorro a Alhama el orden juntamente,
que es luna al fin de vuestro sol ausente.
No quise en la ciudad dormir, que luego
volví a marchar aquella misma tarde,
porque la guerra no admite sosiego
en el valor que nunca fue cobarde.
Del juvenil ardor, del marcial fuego,
el Príncipe, alentado, en el alarde
quiso salir, honrando mi persona
y dejando inmortal vuestra corona,
sobre un polaco de villana raza,
de hermosa vista y de faiciones toscas,
que a corvetas las nubes amenaza,
entre la cola y clin hecho mil roscas,
la piel de la color de la linaza
nevada a trechos de unas blancas moscas
al parecer tan vivas, y a la espuela,
que le han dado las alas con que vuela.
Apenas el bucéfalo villano
escuchó el son de la marcial trompeta,

A fatal skirmish won in hand-to-hand combat
Against our courageous Moorish enemies
Led by the renowned Albayados the Zegri
And his lauded co-commander, Gamal Muza.[52]
Somewhere between the towns of Morón and Ronda,[53]
I dispatched an entire Moorish squadron
With cool contempt and most swift precision –
But getting back to nearby Salamanca:
I found the town sadly lamenting your absence,
Yet my attention was brought back to your prudence,
Your courage, generosity, and spirit
When I shortly learned the urgent reason
That caused your coming here to noble Plasencia:
The timely need to gather men of action
To come to the aid of our forces in Alhama:
That wise command was rising moon, explaining
The absence of your bright and shining sun.
I resolved not to tarry in Salamanca:
I did not sleep one night but went on the march.
War, after all, permits no moment's repose.
The spirited Prince, known for his manly valor,
The lively Prince, who burns with youthful ardor –
Yes, the fiery Don Juan of Asturias
Decided to join in the general muster,
And in so doing, did me the greatest honor
And immortalized your crown forever.
He mounted the most magnificent of steeds –
A fierce one too, of roughest rural breeding.
Threatening the clouds above, he rears up, rises,
Shakes mane and tail, lets loose the fearsome force
Of a hundred thousand thunderous gales,
The severe gray linen of his equine coat,
Flecked with spots of snow, now fully alive.
Man and horse hurtled as one like a wind gust,
Furious spurs from the flapping feet of the former
Giving wings, it seemed, to the flight of the latter.
Barely had the rustic Bucephalus[54]
Perceived the martial blast of the company bugle,

cuando de un mar de espuma crespa cano,
siendo el Príncipe un monte, se inquïeta,
alza el herrado pie, baja la mano,
y da un salto, una coz y una corveta,
midiendo de las casas lo más alto
con la corveta, con la coz y el salto.
   Quiso probar a darle una carrera.
¡Pluguiera a Dios que nunca lo intentara!
Parte el furioso bruto, de manera
que imaginamos que jamás parara.
El vulgo atento el fin violento espera,
que le temió primero que llegara,
que como con su voz Dios le autoriza,
también algunas veces profetiza.
   Cuando en medio de aquesta ligereza,
que al viento, al pensamiento, maravilla,
en su velocidad misma tropieza,
y en el arena pone una rodilla.
Entre las manos mete la cabeza
y a un corcovo le arroja de la silla,
y aunque se asió a los crines, por la frente
cayó sobre los ojos de la gente.
   Levantóse en el vulgo un alarido
mirando la desdicha que temía,
dejarretando al bruto, que corrido
del desmán desdichado se escondía.
Levantamos del suelo sin sentido
al Príncipe don Juan, que ya volvía
en sí animoso, desde allí a la cama,
y marchó luego a socorrer Alhama.
   No se atrevieron a escribir, y quise
de camino avisaros sin pararme,
porque el alarbe bárbaro no pise
el muro que una vez llegó a entregarme.
De su salud confío que os avise
la Infanta doña Juana. Mandad darme

When, from that awesome sea of flowing foam
Upon which the gallant Prince towered and rode
As if upon some rising tidal mountain,
He gets anxious, missteps, lowers massive forelegs,
Leaps in the air, rearing, kicking, nearly reaching
For a moment the heights of houses around him.
Amid all this furious rolling and roiling,
The valiant Prince decides on a running gallop –
How I wish to God he had never tried it!
The beast bolts off with such speed, such force,
We imagined he would never come to a halt.
The thronging crowds, entranced, await violence:
Which, strangely enough, many did anticipate:
Popular opinion may prophesy
Doom and defeat correctly, as if God
Had granted commoners uncommon insight.
Amid this agile, marvelous, heavenly flight,
The hurtling creature stumbles, starts to tumble,
Unwitting victim of its own velocity;
Puts head 'tween forelegs, drops knee to sandy soil,
And gives a tremendous shake of its whole body,
Throwing man from saddle, who though grasping at
The waving manes before him, falls to the ground
In fullest public eye with a sickening thud.
A cry goes out from the crowd: they see before them
The same misfortune they had so long feared.
They launch themselves upon the fleeing beast;
Before it can escape foregone calamity
And disaster, they cut it into pieces.
We gently lifted the Prince up from the ground,
Brought him to a bed, where he came around,
And I marched onward, to Alhama's rescue.
No one dared send a message: I resolved
To bring you the portentous news myself.
But I cannot tarry, no, those barbarous Arabs
Must not tread Alhama's battlements.
Doña Juana, the Infanta, will provide
Updates on the state of her brother's health.[55]

licencia, pues importa la presteza,
y guarde Dios mil años a Su Alteza.

Éntrese tocando las cajas.

ISABEL Para aquí es el valor, Fernando. Agora
es menester el pecho generoso.
FERNANDO Católica Dïana, y vencedora
de tanto cuello alarbe belicoso,
ese heroico valor que España adora,
en tan triste ocasión será forzoso
que se le dé a mi pecho, que en los reyes
del valor quiebra amor las graves leyes.
La fiesta cese aquí, y el Cielo, al ruego
de España, enseñe aquella piedad franca
que siempre nos mostró.
ISABEL Partamos luego,
sin parar en Plasencia, a Salamanca.
FERNANDO Vamos. ¡Sin seso voy de llanto ciego!
ISABEL ¡De sentimiento el alma se me arranca!
GILA Con esto estorbó el Cielo que no huera
dichosa la Serrana de la Vera.

FIN DEL ACTO PRIMERO

Jesús María Josef
Luis Úrsola Francisco Juan Antonio

Give me your leave, time is of the essence.
And may God keep you both a thousand years!

He exits as drums sound.

ISABELLA We have long been known for remarkable valor:
Now is the time for the world to know our hearts.
FERDINAND O Christian Diana, huntress of many an Arab,
You whose courage all of Spain admires –
My heart breaks open upon this sad occasion.
For even the world's most unyielding monarchs,
Love must break the gravest traditions and laws.
The fiesta ends: May Heaven hear our pleas,
And so bestow on Spain the sweet compassion
With which to date it has always kindly graced us.
ISABELLA We leave this very instant for Salamanca.
Our stay here in Plasencia is over.
FERDINAND Let us go. My mind fails me. I weep blindly.
ISABELLA My heart is ripped from my breast.
GILA This fateful event prevents good fortune
From finding La Serrana de la Vera.

END OF ACT ONE

Jesús María Josef
Luis Úrsola, Francisco Juan Antonio[56]

ACTO SEGUNDO

GILA junto al vestuario, asida de la mancera de un arado, como que está arando, y una aguijada en esotra mano, y dice:

GILA ¡Aquí, Naranjo, ah, Bragado,
malas adivas te den!
¡Cejar y dalle también,
o pues si dejo el arado,
la aguijada os he de her
entre los cuernos pedazos!,
que ya conocéis los brazos
que Gila puede tener.
¿Otra vez? ¡Vuelve aquí, loco!
¡Ojo las coces que da!
¿Qué mosca te picó ya?
¡Ah, Bragado, poco a poco,
o que te dé rabia mala!
¡Respingar y a ello! ¡Eso sí,
pues si apaño desde aquí
un guijarro, no habrá bala
que salga de la escopeta
tan recia como saldrá
desde mi brazo! ¡Merá!
¿Qué dïabros te inquïeta?
¡Eso sí!, pues ha de ser
arar y no respingar,
que respingar y no arar
con otra lo podréis her
que sufra menos que yo
condición y pareceres
de alimañas y mujeres.
Al fin, que aunque me formó
el Cielo con ese ser,
ya no podré a mi pesar
dejarlo de confesar
por no parecer mujer,
que es lo que yo más deseo,

ACT TWO

[Act Two, Scene 1. The fields near Garganta la Olla.]

Gila by the dressing room.[57] *She grasps a plough handle, as if she were ploughing. In the other hand, a prod. She says:*

GILA Come on, Old Red! Move it, Patches![58]
Get going, you stupid beasts,
Or I'll choke your cursed throats!
One step forward, two steps back.
You make me drop this plough again,
I'll use this little prod of mine
To smash your stubborn horns to pieces.
You know the strength of Gila's arms.
Not again? This way, idiot!
Watch that kicking! Have you been bitten
By a flea? – Come on, Patches!
Step by step, that's right, my friend
Or I'll whip you into lather!
Fine, go ahead, kick up some dirt,
I'll pick up a cobblestone:
There's no bullet flies with the force
Of what's hurled from my unfurled arm.
What the hell's gotten into you?
Calm down! Yes, that's better.
You're here to plough, not kick up dirt!
Save that behavior for some woman
Willing to put up with you,
Though as they say, horses and women
Share the same hard heads.
Heaven gave me the form you see.
Much to my rage and my distress.
What I desire most in the world
Is not to be seen as a woman.

que el varonil corazón
me dio con esta pensión.
De Garganta la Olla, creo
que torna Mingo.

(De adentro MINGO.)

MINGO ¡Jo, jo!
¡Jo, jo, burra de un bellaco!

Sale MINGO.

GILA ¿Qué hay, Mingo?
MINGO En viéndote aplaco
cualquiera cólera.
GILA Yo
te agradezco la fineza.
¿Qué hay de nuevo en el lugar?
MINGO Mucha noche y desear
el día de tu belleza,
que dempués que estás arando
en el lugar no amanece.
GILA Que vienes de humor parece.
MINGO Vengo, Gila, deseando
ver tus ojos y mirar
las flores que dan tus pies,
y besártelos dempués.
¡Ah, si quisieses amar,
si dieses como las otras
zagalas en dar favores
a sus firmes amadores!
Pero luego te enquillotras
en tratándote de amor,
y no quieres conocer
cómo naciste mujer.
Todo es fiereza y rigor,
todo es matar, y a la he,
Gila, si en mirallo das,
que matan tus ojos más
pero es de amores.

In this toil, my heart is male.
Is that Mingo? Coming out here
From Garganta la Olla?

Mingo offstage.

MINGO (off) Whoa, whoa, you stupid donkey!

Enter Mingo.

GILA What's the matter, Mingo?
MINGO Gila!
Any anger I feel is soothed,
Seeing you.
GILA Very kind of you.
Any news to report from town?
MINGO Just one desolate nighttime,
Desiring your radiant daytime:
Ever since you've been out ploughing,
The dawn never breaks in town.
GILA You're in quite a mood.
MINGO I've come,
Gila, needing to gaze upon
Your eyes, to see the flowers
That blossom in your footsteps,
And then lay my lips upon them.
If only you knew how to love,
If only you granted little favors
Like those other shepherd maidens
Who do what their lovers ask.
Who can trust you when it comes to love?
You refuse to recognize
That you were born a woman.
You're stern, serious, downright murderous,
And you murder me with those eyes
Of yours, you murder me with love.

GILA No sé,
Mingo, lo que has visto en mí
agora más que otras veces.
MINGO Lo que agora me pareces
siempre, Gila, conocí,
mas no he tenido ocasión
de decirte lo que siento,
sino es esta vez que intento
declararte mi pasión.
Y no sé lo que tienen
un hombre y una mujer
a solos que aun sin querer
a mayores cosas vienen.
Dígalo fray Juan Guarín,
y otros muchos, que ha tentado
la soledad, y han gozado
de altas empresas el fin,
que en cuantas mujeres ves
que casi imposibles son,
alcanza más la ocasión
que el amor ni el interés.
¿Aquel cuento no has oído
de aquel rey que por ahí
dicen que estaba de sí
tan loco y desvanecido,
que no pensaba que había
otro hombre crïado el Cielo
más perfeto sobre el suelo,
y estando mirando un día
por los resquicios acaso
de una puerta, descubrió
a la Reina dentro, y vio
que tenía –¡Estraño caso!–,
en los brazos un enano,
escarmiento de señores,
haciéndole mil amores
solo porque le halló a mano,
olvidando la hermosura,

GILA What do you see in me now,
That you didn't see before?
MINGO What I see in you now is what
I've always seen but never had
The chance to say to you before.
I am here to declare my passion.
What do a man and woman
Amount to in this world, alone?
Though they may hardly know it,
They were meant for greater things.
[So said Fray Juan Guarín[59] –
You know him, the famous hermit –
And so said many others who
Attempted solitude and
Sought celibate pursuits.
Besides, when it comes to women who
Are impossible to get,
Opportunity achieves much more,
Opportunity opens doors
Far more than love or money.
Haven't you heard the famous story
Of that king, so crazed and dizzy,
He thought heaven had never placed
On earth a more perfect man?
One day, through the crack of a door,
He spied the queen, who held – o God! –
In her sweet arms, the palace dwarf,
Loving him in a thousand ways,
All because the little guy
Happened to be at hand.
His proximity made her forget

la grandeza y perfeción
del Rey, porque la ocasión
goza de la coyuntura?
Esta ha sido la que a mí,
Gila, me da atrevimiento
de decirte lo que siento.
Ama y volverás por ti,
que viéndote tan hermosa,
tan moza, tan alentada,
tan bien vestida y calzada,
tan discreta, tan airosa,
los que de las quejas suyas
ven que no tienes cuidado
han dicho que los has dejado
por faltas secretas tuyas.
Y bien se ve que han mentido,
porque no pueden caber
en tan hermosa mujer
otras faltas que su olvido.
Ama, Gila, pues que ves
que ama el oso, el jabalí,
el toro, el jumento…

GILA ¿Así
querrás tú?

MINGO Gila, dempués
que te conozco, no soy
señor de mi libertad,
y si va a decir verdad,
tan enquillotrado estoy,
que he de her un disparate
si a la mano no me vas,
adonde nunca jamás,
Gila, me encuentren.

GILA No trate,
pues consiste en mi el remedio
tu amor de temeridades.
Si a amarme te persüades,
y no hay mar ni monte en medio

Her handsome, powerful king.
Let this be a warning to all lords!
Opportunity takes great pleasure
In bringing couples together.
And so I dare, dearest Gila,
To finally tell you how I feel.
Come to your senses. Love. Look at you!
So beautiful, girl-like, glowing,
Gracefully dressed and well shod,
Elegant, uncommonly clever.
As for those sick of your complaining –
Beware, you know what they're saying?
They say that you must be lacking
In certain private womanly parts.
I say, you can prove them wrong.
I say, the only thing she lacks
Is memory of who she was.][60]
So love, Gila, love. Bears do it.
Boars do it. Even the mighty bull.
And as for the humble donkey –
He needs some loving too.

GILA So that's your idea of love?

MINGO Gila, ever since I met you,
I no longer rule my emotions:
I'm so helplessly out of my mind,
If you refuse to take my hand,
I'm bound to commit some rash act
In some place they'll never find me

GILA No need for that course of action.
If I'm the one and only cure
For this fearful love of yours;
If you've decided you must love me
And neither mountain nor sea

que lo estorbe, yo procuro
hacerte, Mingo, favores.
Dime requiebros y amores.

MINGO ¡Gracias al Cielo que el muro
de imposible tan estraño
rindió al amor el desdén!
¡Yo me doy el parabién
y adoro tu desengaño,
pues te alumbró a conocer
la necedad que hasta aquí
has hecho! ¡Yo estoy sin mí,
Gila, de amor y placer!
¿Qué requiebros te diré
que igualen a tu hermosura?
¿Sol? Ya es viejo, y su fegura
no llega, Gila, a tu pie,
que es carirredondo y rojo,
y no tiene pies ni manos.
¿Pues, luna? No es de cristianos,
y es mudable a cada antojo.
¿Estrella? Mirado bien,
es requiebro de Rey Mago.
Si ángel del Cielo te hago,
te vengo a ofender también,
porque no hay ángel nenguno
que menos de cinco mil
años tenga. Pues si abril
de los campos, todo es uno,
porque ha que el abril nació
otros cinco mil también,
y que este nombre te den,
nunca bien me pareció,
porque al más florido prado
suele un jumento atreverse,
y un caminante ponerse
a dejarlo perfumado,
sino es que a tan malhechores
les hacen contradición

Must come between us, then
I will grant you little favors
For your tender words and affections.

MINGO The walls come tumbling down!
Goodbye, disdain! Hello, love!
And if I may say so myself,
I deserve congratulations.
How I worship the revelation
That's led you to see the light
And realize how stupid you've been.
Gila, I am out of my mind,
I explode with love and desire.
What tender words can I offer
Equal to your great beauty?
The sun? It's old. You outshine it.
It's a big, round, red-faced blob
Without arms, legs, or torso.
The moon? More so. Not for Christians:
It is the Moorish symbol.
Besides, the darn thing wanes and waxes.
A star? Well, considered closely, it's
Best extolled by ancient Magi.
I could call you 'heavenly angel'
But I'd do you great offense,
For every angel in the Bible
Is decrepit, five thousand years old.
Same goes for the fields in April:
In fact, you can add another
Five thousand years to get their total.
And even the most flowery meadow
Gets trampled down by some poor donkey
Or perfumed by some traveler
Who leaves his scented offerings.
[To defend them against this crap,

las ortigas, porque son
mesegueros de las flores,
pues si te trueco el cabello
en oro, la tez en plata,
las mejillas de escarlata
en nácar, el blanco cuello
en el más terso marfil,
la roja boca en coral,
y los dientes en cristal,
con el aliento de abril
y otras cosas que aun los rudos
troncos lo publican ya,
para tu beldad será
trocarte, Gila, en menudos,
y siendo tu cuerpo entero
carne y güeso como todos,
herte con estos apodos
aparador de pratero.
Lo que te podré decir
es que le han dado tus ojos
al alma tales antojos,
que la han de her malparir
si antes beber no me dejas
por esa boca penada.
Pero lo que más me agrada,
Gila, en ti son las orejas,
que cada vez que te pinto
acá en la imaginación,
no las hallo, porque son,
Gila, orejas de Corinto,
y si mordellas me dejas,
será favor soberano,
porque tengo el gusto alano
que se me va a las orejas.

GILA ¿Pequeñas te han parecido
mis orejas, y te he dado
plato de orejas, guisado
de que tú solo has comido,
y aún no quedas satisfecho?

Flowers have only the lowly ants.
Yes, were I to invoke the breath
Of April, to turn your hair to gold,
Your complexion to shining silver,
Your scarlet cheeks to purest pearl,
Your lily neck to whitest marble,
Your ruby mouth to reddest coral,
Your bright teeth to sparkling crystal –
Yes, if I could summon every
Elegy proclaimed by every leaf
Dangling from every forest tree,
It would only serve to transform
Your luscious body to worthless fruit.
After all, you are flesh and blood.
Why polish you into silverware
When you're the dish, ready to eat?][61]
Let me simply say, your eyes
Have filled me with such longing that
There will be a miscarriage if
You refuse to let me drink from
The narrow cup of your mouth.
What I like most of all about you
Are your ears – they adorn you like
A pair of teensy, tiny, juicy,
Succulent Corinthian grapes.[62]
Would you let me nibble on them?
It would be the greatest pleasure
To err in the general direction
Of those delectable lobes.

GILA So my ears seem small to you?
I serve them up to you alone,
And still you're wanting more?

MINGO Espero favor mayor,
y es el huego y el amor
de esa condición.
GILA Sospecho
que tomarás una mano
agora si te la doy.
MINGO Y de allí a los pies me voy,
que no quiero ser villano.
Dame a besar su cristal,
su marfil, nieve, su cielo…
GILA Toma.
MINGO ¡Ah, pesar de mi agüelo!
GILA ¿Tanto bien puede hacer mal?
MINGO ¡Que me matas, Gila. ¡Suelta!
GILA Mingo, ¿no ves que te quiero
favorecer?
MINGO ¡Yo no espero
favor de ti…
GILA Estoy resuelta
de que sea esta amistad
apretada entre los dos.
MINGO ¡Afloja, Gila, por Dios,
que yo diré la verdad!
GILA ¿A la primer vuelta cantas
en el tormento, gallina?
MINGO ¡Los güesos me has hecho harina!
GILA ¿De aquesto poco te espantas?
MINGO ¿Esto es poco? ¡Pesia mí,
y me has dejado sin dedos!
GILA ¡Qué bueno para los miedos
que yo he tenido a ti,
viéndome sola contigo,
mujer, y en un despoblado!
MINGO Hoy solo lo has confesado,
pero mi mano es testigo,
aunque no podrá firmallo,
que eres fiera y no mujer,
que eres tenaza en morder

MINGO	I await a greater favor.
Love is like a blazing fire,
Consuming itself without limit.
GILA	You're about to consume my whole hand.
MINGO	From there I'll proceed to the feet,
To bow my head nobly before you.
Let me kiss your snow, your crystal,
Your smooth marble, your gorgeous heaven.
GILA	Take it!
MINGO	Help me, grandfather!
GILA	Doesn't this feel good to you?
MINGO	You're killing me, Gila, let go!
GILA	I'm favoring you, Mingo,
Exactly like you wanted.
MINGO	I wasn't expecting…
GILA	I want
Our friendship to get much, much tighter.
MINGO	Loosen that grip, Gila, by God.
Please, I'm telling you the truth!
GILA	You're clucking at the first turn
Of the wheel, you little hen.
MINGO	You're grinding my bones to flour!
GILA	Wilting already? This is nothing.
MINGO	Nothing? Where are my fingers?!
GILA	Thank you for helping me overcome
Any fear I had of you,
A woman who found herself alone
Out in the middle of nowhere.
MINGO	Now you've made your feelings clear.
[My hand is witness to it all,
Though right now it can't sign off –
Witness that you are no woman
But a wild, raging beast,

y en el aspereza rallo,
albarda en matarme, espuela
en picarme el corazón,
sastre en mentirme afición,
lobo y zorra en la cautela,
mujer en arrepentirte,
escribano en apretar,
cebolla en herme llorar,
vestido viejo en reírte,
suegra en mostrarme rigor,
en la voluntad, cuñado,
en la ingratitud, crïado,
y en las promesas, señor,
memoria en atormentarme,
tiempo en burlarme sotil,
marzo en la cola, alguacil
en prenderme y no soltarme,
en mudanzas, baile y mar,
más tiesa en tu parecer
que de gorra suele ser
el alcalde de un lugar,
en lo zaino, coz, mostaza
en lo huerte, en lo roín,
necio rogado, rocín
en querer ser tu almohaza,
en el sacudirte, galgo,
en maltratar pechos, tos,

Lashing me with talons and
Grating me like I'm a hunk of cheese.
You weigh on me like saddle-bags,
Poke and prod my heart like spurs.
You're a nasty, cheating liar,
You're as loathsome as a tailor,
You're a cunning little monster,
A girly fox, a mangy he-wolf,
Yet when it comes to being trusted,
You're exactly like a woman.
Like a scribe, your words oppress me.
Like an onion, you make me weep.
In your hands, I'm a tattered frock,
You're cruel as a mother-in-law,
Though your lovely attitude would
Make you a fine brother-in-law too.
As for pure ingratitude,
You'd make a perfect servant,
Though for the way you lead me on
With promise after promise you'd
Be an ideal lord and master.
You hound me like a memory,
You rattle me like the month of March,
You mock me like the changing weather,
And pursue me like a sheriff.
As for all your many moods,
You're constant as the open ocean,
Tranquil as a drunken dancer.
You've got the soft and tender looks
Of a village magistrate;
You're a pinch of mustard up the nose,
You kick like a malicious mare,
You're stubborn like a stupid roan,
And you're gentle to the touch
Like a metal grooming comb –
The kind they use on horses!
You're tender like a rabid greyhound,
You get down deep into the chest

en dar pesadumbres, «vos»
de la boca de un hidalgo,
en tener vueltas, espada,
y en nunca tenerlas, vira,
en desdecirte, mentira,
casamiento en ser pesada.
Quédate, que yo me voy
donde jamás vuelva a verte,
aunque voy, Gila, de suerte
que han de darte nuevas hoy
de que me han visto ahorcar.

GILA Vuelve, Mingo, que no quiero
verte morir, pues no espero
ninguna cosa heredar.
Antes pretendo, si gustas,
hacerte favores más
si tú apercebido estás,
que para cosas tan justas
tengo el pecho más humano.

MINGO Ya no quiero más favor,
que me has quitado el amor,
Gila, como con la mano.

Entre MADALENA alborotada.

MADALENA Gila, ¿qué esperas aquí?

GILA ¿Qué hay de nuevo, Madalena?

MADALENA ¡El concejo alborotado,
toda la villa revuelta!

GILA ¿De qué modo?

MADALENA El capitán
que, Gila, con la escopeta
del lugar echaste un día
ha dado al lugar la vuelta
con más de docientos hombres
de compañía, que piensa
satisfacer el agravio
con abrasarnos la tierra.
Por escusar el concejo

	Like a bad cough, you're a 'Hey, you!' From a presumptuous nobleman, You're a twist in the guts from a rusty sword, And like a crossbow you let fly Violence and destruction. You are exactly like marriage: Annoyance and aggravation. Stay right here, I'm going where I'll never have to see you again. Expect to receive news of me Hanging from the nearest tree.
GILA	Mingo! Come back. I don't want To see you dead, to have that Image hanging over my head. I'd prefer to offer you A few more favors, if you're ready.][63] I'll do what feels right and just: A human heart beats inside this breast.
MINGO	I don't want another favor: That hand of yours robbed me of Every last trace of my love.

Enter Madalena, upset.

MADALENA	Gila, what are you waiting for?[64]
GILA	What's the matter, Madalena?
MADALENA	The Village Council's in an uproar, The town is upside down.
GILA	How?
MADALENA	That Captain who you chased from town At rifle point, is back again With a company of more than Two hundred heavily armed men, And he means to avenge the insult by Burning everything to the ground. [The Council, in desperation,

alborotos y revueltas
con los soldados, al campo
les sacaron tres terneras,
veinte carneros, dos vacas,
de pan como el sol –que apenas
entre la nieve y el pan
no hay nenguna diferencia–,
seis fanegas, un corral
de gallinas, ocho espuertas
de longanizas, chorizos
y perniles de la sierra,
muchos cabritos y gansos,
mucha fruta de la Vera
y seis pellejos, sin esto,
de vino que casi tiembla
de edad, tinto y blanco, y tal
que hace hablar en varias lenguas
a los que aprenden sus brindis,
a los que beben su cencia,
y sin esto cien escudos
al capitán porque hiciera
la gente pasar a Cuacos,
a Valdeflor o a La Venta,
a cuyo presente, Gila,
no dieron otra respuesta
que colgar cuanto te he dicho,
sin temor y sin vergüenza
de Dios ni del Rey, del rollo,
como si estas cosas hueran
ladrones o pesos falsos,
y entrársenos por las puertas.
Entró el Capitán delante,
todo plumas, la jineta
en la mano, y un mochacho
que le lleva una rodela,
todos tras él disparando
de cinco en cinco en hilera,
y al son de los atambores,

Is trying to make things right
With the soldiers – they brought three calves
To the fields where they're camped,
Along with twenty head of steer;
Two dairy cows; an enormous
Quantity of fresh, hot bread;
Six bushels of our best wheat;
An entire coop of hens;
Eight large bags stuffed with sausage,
Chorizo, jamón serrano;
Dozens of goats, wheels of cheese;
The finest fruit of La Vera;
Six skins brimming with wine,
So fine, it trembles with age –
Both red and white, I should say,
The kind that causes tongues to toast
With oratory of the most
Subtle and refined turns of phrase.
And if all that weren't enough,
They gave the Captain and his men
One hundred shields emblazoned with
Our local coat of arms to
Provide them with safe passage through
Cuacos, Valdeflor and La Venta.
To these many offerings,
The soldiers gave no other reply
Than to note it all on a list
Without shame or fear of God
Or King, as if these gracious gifts
Were no more than counterfeit coins.
Then we went back into town.][65]
The Captain entered town first,
Finely dressed, with tasseled spear,
And servant boy to bear his shield.
Everyone else followed behind,
Firing off arms, five by five.
Then, to the sudden beat of drums,

plumas dando, haciendo piernas,
uno con una alabarda,
dando carreras y vueltas
como procesión los rige,
y el que lleva la bandera
la va tremolando al aire,
que es de más colores hecha
que el pendón de un sastre, toda
llena de cifras y letras,
que, según el sacristán,
que es astrólogo y poeta,
leyó desde el campanario,
ha dicho que dice en ellas:
«Gila y Lucas».

GILA Mal la cifra
con el intento concierta
si son muestras de amor
y esotras de nuestra ofensa.

MADALENA Después que pasaron todos,
otra compañía llega
de mujeres que llevaban,
que también van a la guerra,
todas puestas de camino
y en jumentos caballeras,
más afeitadas de cara
que una casa de una aldea.
A la de tu padre, Gila,
llegaron de esta manera,
no sé con qué intento, prima.
Solo sé que mandó apriesa
cerrar las puertas, y yo,
por una falsa pequeña
que al campo sale, he venido
corriendo a darte estas nuevas.

GILA ¡Oh, pesar de mi descuido
que dejase mi escopeta
en casa esta vez! Mas vaya,
que no importa mientras lleva

All was pomp and circumstance:
One man with a battle axe
Ran back and forth to guide the march
While another waved a flag,
A swirl of more color and fabric than
The shelves of any tailor's shop.
This flag brimmed with inscriptions,
Boldly embroidered, brightly lettered.
Our sexton, who is widely known
As poet and astrologer,
Could clearly glean the meaning from
The bell tower of our church.
He said the inscription simply read:
'Gila and Lucas.'

GILA If it's meant
To be a token of love, then
That presumptuous inscription
Badly matches my intention.
In fact, it does us offense.

MADALENA After everyone passed by,
Another company arrived.
These were women they brought along,
Also on their way to war,
Female knights, clomping on mule-back,
Garish faces done up more brightly
Than a freshly white-washed house.
They all arrived at your father's home,
Who knows with what intention.
Cousin, I only know that an order
Was quickly given by your father
To lock every single door.
I slipped out through the back entrance,
The way that leads to the country,
And came running with this news.

GILA And I left my rifle at home!
But no worries, Gila's here,

Gila a sí mesma consigo,
y esta honda y cuatro piedras,
que suele, si al aire escupe,
hacer temblar esta sierra.
Mete, Mingo, en el corral
esos bueyes, y esa reja
guarda en el cortijo, y vamos,
que allá te aguardo.

MINGO Eso huera
a no tener miedo yo.

GILA ¡Vive el Cielo, Madalena,
que han de saber hoy quién es
la Serrana de la Vera!

Vanse.

Entre GIRALDO solo, tocando adentro la caja.

GIRALDO Abre de par en par, Pascual, las puertas,
y el señor Capitán entre en buen hora.
Veamos qué pretende de mi casa,
que reyes, a Dios gracias, y justicia
tenemos para agravios semejantes.

Entre el CAPITÁN

CAPITÁN Hagan alto a la puerta de esta casa,
hasta que avise yo, señor Sargento.

De adentro.

¡Alto de mano en mano! ¡Alto, alto!

GIRALDO Aquí está el dueño de esta casa humilde.
El señor Capitán haga en mí y ella
cuanto gusto le diere, pero mire
que hay Dios y que hay justicia.

CAPITÁN Alzad, Giraldo,
que no vengo a ofenderos sino a daros
ocasión de que honréis la sangre vuestra.

GIRALDO De la nobleza que tenéis dais muestra.
Pero, ¿cómo, señor, queréis que piense
que me venís a honrar de esta manera,

	With her four stones and slingshot: When I spit them in the air, The whole earth quakes and trembles. Mingo, go corral these oxen. Put this ploughshare in the shed. I'll wait for you there. Let's go.
MINGO	I would if I weren't terrified.
GILA	Heaven help them, Madalena, They're about to get to know La Serrana de la Vera.

They exit.

[Act Two, Scene 2. Garganta la Olla. The threshold of Giraldo's house.]

Enter Giraldo, alone, with drums playing offstage.

GIRALDO	Go, throw our doors wide open, Pascual.[66] The Captain is most welcome to come right in. Let's see just what he wants from our household. Thanks be to God, we have a pair of monarchs To protect us from such vicious insults.

Enter the Captain.

CAPTAIN	Have everyone halt at the door of this house, Sergeant, Until you hear me give further command.

Off stage:

[VOICES OFF]	Spread word down the line. Company halt!
GIRALDO	The lord and master of this humble household Stands before you, Captain, at your service. Do with us what you please, but take note: There is a God and there is also justice.
CAPTAIN	Lift yourself from the ground, Giraldo, I am not here to do you any offense, But only to take this opportunity To do fitting honor to your family blood.
GIRALDO	You're showing signs of your nobility But is this how you mean to honor me?

sacándome las puertas de los quicios
para entrar en mi casa?

CAPITÁN Con intento
de lo que digo ha sido. Estadme atento.
Ya estaréis de mi sangre satisfecho
primeramente.

GIRALDO Vuestra noble sangre
es la más noble de Plasencia, y creo
que a vuestro padre conocí, y aun fuera
de vuestro padre, a vuestro agüelo y todo,
que fueron valerosos caballeros.

CAPITÁN Pues yo pretendo honraros con haceros,
Giraldo, padre mío.

GIRALDO ¿De qué modo?

CAPITÁN Si sois mi padre vos, cosa es bien clara
que a Gila quiero por mi esposa.

GIRALDO Agora
digo, señor don Lucas, perdonadme,
que no venís a honrarme, sino solo
a burlaros de mí.

CAPITÁN Giraldo, amigo,
veras son, y muy veras las que os digo.

GIRALDO Gila no es para vos, señor don Lucas,
que es una labradora, hija de un hombre
llano y humilde, aunque de limpia sangre,
rica para el lugar donde ha nacido,
pero no para vos, que sois tan noble.
Buscad una señora que os iguale,
que Gila para vos muy poco vale.

CAPITÁN Antes de su valor, Giraldo, nace
el pretendella yo, que su hermosura
y su valor me tienen inclinado
de tal manera, que ninguna cosa
será causa a poder de esto apartarme,
y esta ha sido también la que me obliga
a venir como veis a vuestra casa
y a Garganta la Olla, porque tengo
patente general para alojarme

Forcing open the doors of my own home?
CAPTAIN My purpose is precisely what I've promised.
Listen carefully, so you'll be satisfied
As to the quality of my family blood.
GIRALDO Your blood is the very noblest in Plasencia.
I do believe I met your father once,
And as for your grandfather, and his father too –
All of them were fine and valiant gentlemen.[67]
CAPTAIN When it comes to fathers, I intend
To honor you by making you my father.
GIRALDO What do you mean?
CAPTAIN Exactly what you have just heard,
My father: I want Gila as my wife.
GIRALDO Then, señor Don Lucas, I beg your pardon:
You come not to honor but to mock me.
CAPTAIN Giraldo, dear friend, all of this is true.
I speak only the sincerest things to you.
GIRALDO Gila's not for you, señor Don Lucas.
She's a villager, a farm girl, daughter
Of the simple humble man before you,
Though proud to possess the purest blood there is.
Yes, she's rich, but only for this village,
Not alongside a nobleman like you.
Find yourself a lady who is your equal:
Gila's worth so little to a man like you.
CAPTAIN I measure her worth by how much I want her.
I measure it by her courage and beauty,
And nothing can make me relinquish such treasure.
That's why I'm back in Garganta la Olla.
That's why I've come to pay this special visit.
What's more, I now have executive patent

por todos los lugares de la Vera.
Solo este bien de vos mi dicha espera.
Gila ha de ser mi esposa, y vos mi padre,
que, ¿qué madre mejor puedo a mis hijos
darles que una mujer que es tan famosa?
No repliquéis palabra, sino dadme
las manos a besar, y háganse luego
las escrituras, que la hacienda vuestra,
con la poca que tengo de mis padres,
ayudarán para pasar, Giraldo,
en Plasencia muy bien cuando yo quiera
dejar la guerra y retirarme a vida
más sosegada y menos divertida.

GIRALDO Ya fuera necedad y grosería
no admitir la merced, señor don Lucas,
que hacéis a Gila y a mi sangre. Digo
que cuanto yo tuviere es vuestro todo,
y no será tan poco que no sea
para pasar muy bien en cualquier parte,
aunque colguéis la azada y los arados.
Y hágaos el Cielo, amén, buenos casados.

CAPITÁN Dadme la mano como padre, y luego
a Plasencia enviaré para que traigan
las amonestaciones, que con una
desposarnos podremos. Y esto sea
con el mayor silencio que pudiéramos
porque mis deudos no lo contradigan.

GIRALDO Disponéis como cuerdo vuestras cosas.
Dadme los brazos, que mi hacienda es vuestra,
mi honor, mi Gila, y vuestra compañía
alójese en mi casa toda junta,
y vos, haced y deshaced en ella,
que estoy loco de gusto, porque días
tan alegres los padres enloquecen.

CAPITÁN Mis nobles pensamientos lo merecen.

GIRALDO Para que vayan a llamar a Gila
me dad licencia, porque está en la arada,
si va a decir verdad.

To lodge myself anywhere in La Vera.
I only await your kindness and your blessing.
You will be my father, Gila will be my wife.
Can the world offer my children a better mother?
I do not need a single word to pass your lips,
I simply need your kindly hands, to kiss.
Go ahead, let's have the legal deeds drawn up.
When we combine your generous rural estate
With what little I myself inherit,
The totality will help me pass my days
In great comfort, in my Plasencia,
On such a day when I surrender arms
And retire to a life of peace.[68]

GIRALDO It would be foolish or rude of me, Don Lucas,
To reject these mercies you show me and Gila.
I say – everything I have is yours.
May it serve to support you generously
Wherever you might be, and allow you
To hang up the proverbial hoe and plough.
May heaven make you the happiest of couples.

CAPTAIN Give me your hand – the hand of a loving father.
I'll send immediately to Plasencia
For the marriage banns. One will suffice.
Let it all be done in the greatest of silence
So no one in my clan dare speak against it.

GIRALDO Take care of your family business as you see fit.
My estate, my honor, my Gila: they are yours,
And your company can quarter under my roof:
I give them free rein of the entire house.
I am out of my mind with pleasure: such moments
Drive fathers crazy with joy.

CAPTAIN You do me honor.

GIRALDO Give me a moment, Captain, to call Gila.
To tell the truth – she's out in the fields, ploughing.

CAPITÁN Del mismo modo
que salió de ella para rey de España
Vamba, puedo estimar que salga Gila,
Giraldo, para reina de mi alma.

GIRALDO Razones son de vuestro heroico pecho.
Volvé a abrazarme.

CAPITÁN Muy en hora buena.

Entre GILA con la honda en la mano, y en ella puesta una piedra, y MADALENA con ella.

GILA ¿Es esto lo que dices, Madalena?

MADALENA Todo el rigor se convirtió en abrazos.

GILA Yo he echado a perder hoy la mayor cólera
que he tenido en mi vida.

GIRALDO ¡Gila!

GILA ¡Padre!

GIRALDO Muy bienvenida seas.

GILA Yo venía
más belicosa que era necesario
para lo que he hallado, pues los brazos
señal de amistad son. Adiós, que quiero
a la arada tornar como primero.

GIRALDO Vuelve acá, Gila. Mira que te aguardan,
con la dicha mayor que mujer tuvo
el Cielo y la Fortuna.

GILA ¿Hanme elegido
por general, por rey, obispo o papa?
¿He heredado las casas, las haciendas,
de los señores de Castilla? ¿Vienen
por mí para Gran Turca bautizada?
¿Llámanme para herme prencipesa
de Castilla y León, o Preste Juana
de las Indias, del Cairo gran señora,
o de Alimaña y Roma emperadora?

GIRALDO Muy altos son tus pensamientos, Gila.

GILA Pedilde, padre, cuenta a las estrellas
de esa altivez, pues ellas son la causa.

CAPTAIN Just like the celebrated old King Wamba,
Who gave up the plough to rule all of Hispania.[69]
In surrendering her plough, may lovely Gila
Become my queen and reign over my heart.
GIRLADO Noble thoughts indeed from your heroic breast!
Embrace me again, son!
CAPTAIN With pleasure, father.

Enter Gila with the loaded slingshot in her hand, and Madalena with her.

GILA This is what you told me about, Madalena?
MADALENA All that terror, transformed into embraces!
GILA And so the greatest rage I've ever felt
Fades as well.
GIRALDO Gila!
GILA Father!
GIRALDO Glad you're here.
GILA I came more prepared to fight a war
Than it seems the circumstances called for.
What do I find? Signs of friendship. Embraces.
Goodbye. I'm back to my plough.
GIRALDO Come back, Gila.
See how fortune favors you, how heaven
Grants you the greatest blessing given a woman.
GILA Have they chosen me to be General?
Elected me monarch, bishop, or Pope?
Am I to inherit every estate in sight?
Named heir apparent to Castile and Leon?
Will I be empress of Constantinople?
Or the world's next Prester 'Juana' to rule
The wide Indies and all oceans between?[70]
What about Germany? The Roman empire?
And will I reign as well over the mighty Nile?
GIRALDO Your thoughts are certainly soaring, Gila.
GILA If they soar, you may blame it on the stars.
They are the cause.

GIRALDO Medir con la humildad del nacimiento,
Gila, la voluntad y el pensamiento.
GILA ¿Qué dicha, padre, al fin es la que aguardo
del Cielo y la Fortuna?
GIRALDO Tu remedio.
GILA ¿Pues qué? ¿Quieres casarme?
GIRALDO Sí, y advierte
si es dicha la que aguardas, pues te caso
con el señor don Lucas, caballero
de los Carvajales de Plasencia,
y juntamente capitán, que a solo
este efeto, no más, Gila, ha venido
a Garganta la Olla.
GILA Hasta agora
me imaginaba, padre, por las cosas
que yo me he visto her hombre, y muy hombre,
y agora echo de ver, pues que me tratas
casamiento con este caballero,
que soy mujer, que para tanto daño
ha sido mi desdicha el desengaño.
No me quiero casar, padre, que creo
que mientras no me caso que soy hombre.
No quiero ver que nadie me sujete.
No quiero que ninguno se imagine
dueño de mí. La libertad pretendo.
El señor Capitán busque en Plasencia
mujer de su nobleza que le iguale,
que yo soy una triste labradora,
muy diferente de él, para los campos
buena, que me conocen, y no quiero
meterme agora a caballera y herme
mujer de piedra en lo espetado y tieso,
encaramada en dos chapines, padre,
y con un verdugado hecha campana,
lominaria con una lechuguilla,
aprendiendo de nuevo reverencias,
que será para mí darme ponzoña,
y Gila no es buen nombre para doña.

GIRALDO Measure your desires,
Daughter, against your plain and humble birth.
GILA Then tell me already, what good fortune awaits me?
GIRALDO The answer to all your woes.
GILA And what can that be?
Do you mean to marry me?
GIRALDO I do, daughter,
And if you desire proof of your good fortune,
Before you is the very man in question:
A gentleman, a captain, and a Carvajal.
He's come expressly for this special purpose.
GILA Until this moment, father, I had always
Seen myself as a man, and very much one.
But now I perceive, with this proposed marriage,
I am forced to become a woman.
This disillusion is my grave misfortune,
My suffering. I do not want to marry.
As long as I am unwed, I remain a man.
I aspire to be free. I cannot imagine
Anyone subjecting or subduing me.
No man on earth shall think himself my master.
Let the señor go back to Plasencia,
I'm sure he can find a woman there his equal.
I'm a mere farm girl, made for the fields,
I don't see myself getting raised up on heels,
Becoming a fine lady, rigid, erect,
Flouncing around in endless layered petticoats,
Some bulbous church bell, billowing and bloated,
Transformed beneath a suffocating ruff
Into a human lampshade; having to learn
All the tedious courtesies from scratch.
Better to make me drink poison. Besides,
Gila is no kind of name for a Doña.[71]

CAPITÁN No es bien que despreciéis, hermoso dueño,
de mis deseos y del alma mía,
–Perdóneme Giraldo, vuestro padre,
que desde aquí le tengo ya por mío–,
amor que se reduce a pensamientos
tan bien nacidos, tan en honra vuestra,
que, por vida de vuestros dos luceros,
ojos del cielo de esa hermosa cara,
que habéis de ser al lado de don Lucas,
si merezco esa mano, otra Semíramis,
otra Evadnes y Palas española.
GILA Esa razón me puede obligar sola,
por imitar a vuestro lado luego
a la gran Isabel, que al de Fernando
emprende heroicos hechos, que si vivo,
y ocasiones me ofrece la Fortuna,
ha de quedar contra la edad ligera
fama de la Serrana de la Vera.
CAPITÁN Pedidme albricias porque os dé deseos
nuevos, almas y vidas con que amaros.
GILA Aunque no supe amor, pienso pagaros.
MADALENA Goza el estado muchos años, Gila.
GILA Será para servirte, Madalena.

DON GARCÍA, de camino.

DON GARCÍA Nunca en la Vera imaginé alcanzaros.
CAPITÁN Seáis muy bienvenido, don García,
que habéis estado, a fe, bien deseado.
¿Cómo habéis, en efeto, despachado?
DON GARCÍA Luego en llegando me aprobó el Consejo,
aunque llegué a ocasión a Salamanca
para España bien trágica.

CAPTAIN It's not right for you to overlook
The love I feel for you: you are mistress
Of my deepest longings and desires –
May your father excuse this show of candor,
But in my heart she is already mine.
These sentiments, born of purest intention,
Only mean to honor these two morning stars,
Shining gorgeously from the rare heaven
Of this stunning and celestial face.
You are meant to be at Don Lucas's side,
If he prove worthy of your perfect hand.
Yes, you are meant be a Semiramis,
A latter-day Evadne, a Pallas Athena,
A powerful warrior come to grace our Spain.[72]

GILA That is the one and only reason, señor,
I can ever consent to be at your side:
To imitate our great Queen Isabella,
Who alongside her noble partner Ferdinand
Undertakes the most heroic deeds.
May I live to see the day when fortune
Offers me opportunity to achieve
Such lasting fame, so that the name of
La Serrana de la Vera outlasts the
Flight of time itself.

CAPTAIN Then let me fulfill this hope:
I offer hearts and souls and new desires
All in service to this love of you.

GILA Though I know nothing of the ways of love,
I hope I can find some way to repay you.

MADALENA Many happy years to you!

GILA I hope to serve you too.

Enter Don García, in travelling clothes.

DON GARCÍA I never thought I'd find you in La Vera.

CAPTAIN Welcome, Don García. We've greatly missed you.
Did you manage to take care of business?[73]

DON GARCÍA The Royal Council granted their full approval
The moment that I arrived in Salamanca,
Despite the tragic circumstances for Spain.

CAPITÁN ¿En que estado
queda el Príncipe?
DON GARCÍA Oídme con cuidado.
Después que de la carrera
de aquel caballo que a España
fue el de Troya, pues ha sido
de tan gran desdicha causa,
quedó el Príncipe don Juan
tan enfermo en Salamanca
de su mal lograda vida
con tan pocas esperanzas,
Fernando y doña Isabel,
la jornada de Granada
dejando, dieron la vuelta
a llorar tan gran desgracia.
Siete dotores lo curan,
y entre ellos de la Parra,
nuevo Galeno español
que a Esculapio se adelanta.
Todos hasta el catorceno
la vida al Príncipe alargan,
y el de la Parra una noche
le dice tales palabras:
«Muy malo está Vuestra Alteza,
don Juan, príncipe de España.
Al cuerpo faltan remedios,
acúdanse a los del alma.
La muerte a nadie perdona,
que de los reyes las guardas
atropella y no respeta,
como mayor rey la manda.
Tres horas tenéis de vida,
y la una ya se pasa,
que de la vida es el pulso
el reloj que las señala.
Quien os engaña no os quiere,
y a quien hoy os desengaña
debéis más, que las lisonjas

CAPTAIN How is the Prince?

DON GARCÍA Listen carefully.[74]

The infamous incident
Of the runaway horse –
A Trojan horse, to be sure,
For the ruin it brought to Spain –
Led Prince Don Juan to languish
Hopelessly in Salamanca,
And Ferdinand and Isabella
To weep over this misfortune,
Interrupting their journey
To the Granada campaign.
Seven doctors attended him,
Among them the famed de la Parra,
That Spanish Galen who outshines
The great Asclepius himself.[75]
For fourteen days and fourteen nights
They extended the Prince's life.
Then, one evening, de la Parra
Pronounced these fateful words:
'Your Highness Don Juan, Prince of Spain,
Is now in the gravest condition.
No more cures remain for the body,
Attend to those of the soul.
Death pardons no one in its course.
It tramples mighty monarchs
And ignores commands of kings.
You have three hours left to live,
And the first is fast ticking away.
Thus all our lives ebb as they pulse;
He who tells you otherwise
Does not love you, good Prince;
He who strips illusions from you
Places you in eternal debt.

aquí no sirven de nada.
Sin herederos vos deja
el Cielo. Secretas causas
debe de haber que lo ordenan
que en la tierra no se alcanzan.
El reino, por vuestra muerte,
queda a la señora Infanta.
Ampare Dios a Castilla,
y a vos os perdone el alma.»
Valor mostrando, responde
el Príncipe al de la Parra:
«Con ser la verdad primera
que me han dicho, no me espanta.
Natural cosa es la muerte.
Solo me aflige la falta
que puedo hacer a Castilla,
aunque dejo tres hermanas.
Pero Dios, que determina
que muera, sabrá amparalla
con herederos que importen
más a su iglesia romana.»
Y recibiendo de nuevo
los sacramentos, dio el alma
al Cielo, luto a Castilla
y general llanto a España.
En la catedral se hizo
un túmulo, cuya rara
fábrica admiró en su pompa
la arquitectura romana.
El edificio soberbio
las cuatro especies mostraba
de las colunas antiguas
que inventó Efesio y Acaya,
las dóricas y corintias,
las jónicas y tuscanias,
que el español mauseolo
hasta los cielos levantan
sobre los embasamentos

Flattery means nothing now.
Heaven leaves you without heirs
For reasons we here on earth
Are fated never to know.
The kingdom falls to the Infanta.[76]
May God protect Castile
Forever, and pardon your soul.'
The prince, showing courage, answered:
'This is the first truthful thing
Anyone has said to me.
Death is natural. I have no fear.
I grieve only for leaving my Castile
Three siblings, all of them sisters.[77]
But since God determines
That I must die, I trust He will
Find a way to protect this land
With heirs that are acceptable
To the holy Roman church.'
Thus receiving final sacraments,
His soul was given to heaven,
And Castile was draped in mourning,
And all Spain exploded in tears.
A grand sepulchral monument
Was erected in the cathedral,
Its extraordinary form
Rivaling the architecture
Of ancient Rome in pomp and glory.
The impressive edifice
Featured all four columns known
To Arcady and Ephesus:[78]
The Corinthian and Doric,
The Tuscan and Ionic.
Thus the Spanish mausoleum
Skyward soared on pedestals

de pedestales y basas,
cuadros, equinos, boceles,
lengüetas escitas, zanjas,
nacelas, filetes, plintos,
murecillos, contrabasas,
troquilos, planos, talones,
armilas, gradillas, bandas,
cuyo hermoso frontispicio
con el capitel rematan
arquitrabes y cornijas,
frisas y molduras varias,
coronas, gulas, casetos,
gotas, balaústres, armas,
ejes, triglifos, metopas,
témpanos, linteles, jambas.
Tocaba el capelardente
en la cúpula musaica
de la capilla mayor,
adonde un águila estaba
al sol probando sus hijos,
y uno de ellos con las alas
batiendo sus rayos de oro
con unas letras doradas
que dicen: «Este es mi nido.
Adiós, grandezas humanas,
que parecéis muy pequeñas
desde tan alto miradas.»
Doce pendones pendían
luego en las castellanas
y aragonesas insinias,
y en el capitel, España,
armada como la pintan,
pisando yelmos y espadas,
cuyas lágrimas son letras
que de esta suerte lloraban:

Of the finest fascias and plinths.
Amongst the moldings, there were torus,
Astragal and cyma –
Flush, fluted, and filleted;
There were pediments, pilasters,
Peristyles, ramp-ways, risers;
The most serene of surfaces,
Their fore parts finished with
Architraves and cornices;
There were friezes and ornaments
Of all kinds, rounded and floral;
Entablatures, stylobates,
Balustrades, triglyphs, metopes,
Tympanum, vertical axes,
Dintels, lintels, abaci.[79]
The monumental tomb itself,
With myriad candles aglow,
Almost grazed the high mosaics
That crowned the central chapel.
A proud eagle perched atop it,
Showing its children to the sun.
One of these figures, wings beating
On a billow of golden rays,
Proclaimed in gilded lettering:
'This is my nest. Farewell to all
Human achievement, so small
It seems when seen from heights like these.'
Twelve great banners were then unfurled
Bearing the insignias
Of Castile and Aragon,
And on the highest capital
Of all, there loomed the famous
Insignia of our
Imperial Spanish nation,
Martial and victorious,
Weeping tears in torrents,
Tears that in turn became letters,
Letters which spelled out these words:

«Yo he perdido solamente,
que el Príncipe don Juan gana
más dichosas monarquías,
conquistas más soberanas.»
Al lado derecho suyo
estaba también la Fama,
y al siniestro la Fortuna,
que rendida se mostraba,
y más abajo, la Muerte,
arrepentida y turbada,
reclinando el flaco cuerpo
sobre su corva guadaña.
En medio de este edificio
que ardiendo en luces estaba,
el del Príncipe pusieron,
armado con blancas armas,
la corona en la cabeza,
puesta la mano en la espada,
dando ocasión a los ojos
que con lágrimas cegaran.
Mostrando el valor que tienen,
los católicos monarcas
a las obsequias asisten,
y luego, en siendo acabadas,
los monteros de Espinosa
el cuerpo en hombros levantan
y a la bóveda le llevan,
donde un secretario aguarda,
que toma por testimonio
que queda en aquella caja
de plomo el cuerpo. Y con esto
todos los actos se acaban,
previniendo el juramento
de la Infanta doña Juana
–Que mil años guarde el Cielo,
como ha menester España–.

CAPITÁN Notable desgracia ha sido.

GIRALDO Toda esta vida es desgracias.

'I suffer this great loss here on earth
So Prince Don Juan may go on to
Greater victories in heaven.'
To its right was Fame herself.
To its left was Lady Fortune,
Posed in posture of surrender.
Below it, Death, regretful,
Its withered body reclining on
A sleek, curvaceous scythe.
In the center of this edifice,
Torches blazing all around,
They placed the Prince's tomb.
He was laid out in his armor,
The crown upon his head,
And sword in hand, so as to blind
All eyes in untold tears and grief.
Our monarchs showed great courage
In attending to these rites.
Once concluded, the royal guard,
The Monteros de Espinosa,[80]
Bore the body on their shoulders
And brought it down to the vaults.
There a scribe awaited them,
Who took the box's leaden weight as
Testimony to the Prince's fate.
Thus concluded the ceremonies,
Thus we'll wait upon the oath of
The Infanta Doña Juana.
Spain now badly needs her.
May heaven protect her always.[81]

CAPTAIN How tragic.

GIRALDO Life is tragic.

GILA Las lágrimas, Madalena,
de lástima se me saltan.
MADALENA No te he visto jamás tierna,
sino es hoy.
GILA La misma causa
trae consigo el llanto, prima.
CAPITÁN Hay novedades estrañas.
DON GARCÍA ¿Dónde ha de estar la bandera?
CAPITÁN Aquí, que el cuerpo de guardia
quiere Giraldo que sea
dentro de su misma casa.
Vamos a alojar la gente.
Adiós, Giraldo
GIRALDO Dios vaya
con vos.
GILA Adiós, dueño mío.
CAPITÁN Él mismo os guarde.
DON GARCÍA No es mala,
don Lucas, la motilona.
CAPITÁN ¡A Gila le dejo el alma!

Vanse DON LUCAS y DON GARCÍA.

GIRALDO Aliña la casa, Gila,
y haz que se pongan dos camas
para el Capitán y Alférez.
Las sábanas nuevas saca
de tu ajüar, y las colchas,
y enfunda cuatro almohadas,
que no güela más que a limpio
todo, y quita de la sala
los ciegayernos, que agora
solo los ciega tu cara
y tu varonil valor,
que es la dote que te casa.
Y a los capones más gordos
tuerce los cuellos, y mata
un lechón, y arroja dentro
de la olla dos torcazas

GILA Tears pour from me uncontrollably.
MADALENA I've never seen you so tender, cousin.
GILA It stems from that same grief, cousin.
CAPTAIN What fateful news.
DON GARCÍA Captain,
Where do we hoist the flag?
CAPTAIN Right here.
Giraldo wishes us to make
Our headquarters inside his home.
Let's start quartering the men.
Goodbye, Giraldo
GIRALDO God go with you.
CAPTAIN Goodbye, mistress of my heart.
GILA God go with you, Captain.
DON GARCÍA The wench isn't half bad, Don Lucas.
CAPTAIN I leave my heart with Gila.

Exit Don Lucas and Don García.

GIRALDO Gila, get the house prepared.
Make sure two beds are made up
For the Captain and Lieutenant.
Take out the new sheets and coverlets
And stuff four good pillows with down.
Everything must smell clean and fresh.
Clear away all those knick-knacks,
Nothing should obscure his view
Of your face and manly spirit:
Let him get the knack of that for
That's the only dowry you have.
Find the fattest capons and
Wring their necks. Kill a suckling pig.

palomas y algún sisón,
que de lo que toca a vaca
y carnero buena queda.
Y mientras voy a la plaza,
pon la mesa, y queda a Dios.

Vase GIRALDO

MADALENA Prima Gila, ordena y manda,
que yo te ayudaré a todo.
GILA Vamos primero que nada
a ver del modo que ponen,
prima, la bandera y armas.
MADALENA Soldados salen aquí
a jugar, si no me engaña,
Gila, la maginación,
los dados sobre una caja,
que así suelen herlo siempre.
GILA De buena gana jugara,
prima, los dados con ellos.
MADALENA ¿Sabes?
GILA Cuando estuvo en casa
del barbero la bandera
el año pasado, daba
en mirar y aprendí el juego.
MADALENA Todo cuanto hay se te alcanza.
GILA Por inclinación soy hombre.

Salgan ANDRÉS y GERÓMINO y OTRO SOLDADO, con una caja y dados para jugar.

ANDRÉS El socorro huego.
GERÓNIMO ¡Vaya!
ANDRÉS ¡Que me ha picado, por Dios,
el señor Cabo de Escuadra!
CABO Pues adviértole que luego
muda la posta de guarda.
ANDRÉS Dorabuena.
GERÓNIMO Más al once.
ANDRÉS Esto paro a la trocada.

Toss two pigeons and a moor-cock
Into a pan of sizzling oil.
Make sure there's plenty of beef
And mutton. Set the table.
I'm going out to the plaza.
That's all. Goodbye.

Exit GIRALDO

MADALENA Tell me how I can help, cousin.
GILA First and foremost, let's go watch them
Hoist the flag and set up arms.
MADALENA Soldiers are showing up to gamble.
They're rolling dice on a box,
The way I've seen soldiers do.
GILA I'd love to join them.
MADALENA You know how?
GILA Remember when they flew the banner
From the barber's house last year?
I watched them, and I learned.
MADALENA Nothing escapes your notice, Gila.
GILA I'm inclined to be a man.

Enter Andrés and Gerónimo and another soldier [the Corporal] with a box and dice.

ANDRÉS I'm staking all my wages.
GERÓNIMO All right!
ANDRÉS God help me, our corporal
Is up my ass!
CORPORAL Take good note:
We're changing headquarters.
ANDRÉS Here we go.
GERÓNIMO Elevens again.
ANDRÉS That's how they tumble.

GERÓNIMO Tire, que un once ganó.
ANDRÉS ¡Oh, cuatro veces mal haya
quien es desdichado y juega!

(Lléganse a ver jugar GILA y MADALENA. Saca el dinero y pónelo en la mesa y toma los dados.)

CABO ¿Quiere jugar, camarada?
GILA De buena gana por cierto
yo juego.
CABO ¿Hay dinero?
GILA En plata.
CABO ¡Moza varonil, por Dios!
ANDRÉS Gerónimo, la Serrana
es esta que allí en Plasencia...
Ya te acuerdas.
GERÓNIMO ¿Pues no basta
para memoria los toques
que contra negras y blancas
espadas nos dio a los dos
con sola una negra espada?
Su casa pienso que es esta.
ANDRÉS Desimula agora y calla,
que antes de marchar un chirlo
le ha de quedar por la cara.
GILA ¿No juegan?
ANDRÉS Pues ¿por qué no?
GILA A todos digo.
GERÓNIMO Quien paga
tan francamente no es mucho
que lo diga.
CABO A todos gana.
ANDRÉS Sino es a mí, que no quiero.
GILA De barato se lo daba
si no hubiera puesto encima
la mano.
ANDRÉS Las suyas blancas
beso por esa merced,
pero aténgome a mis garras.

GERÓNIMO Elevens wins.
Roll again.
ANDRÉS Why the hell am I
Always cursed with rotten luck?

(Gila and Madalena come over to observe the gambling.)

CORPORAL You want to play, little lady?
GILA Absolutely I want to play.
CORPORAL You've got money?
GILA In silver.

(Gila takes out money and puts it on the table and grabs the dice.)

CORPORAL God help me, it's a He-Girl!
ANDRÉS Gerónimo, that's her,
The serrana in Plasencia….
Remember?
GERÓNIMO How can I forget
The way she touched us up with her sword?
I think she lives in this house.
ANDRÉS Shut up, smile, and watch me
Carve a permanent grin
Into her lovely, little face.
GILA You won't play with me?
ANDRÉS What's that to you?
GILA I'm talking to everyone.
GERÓNIMO Just because you lay out money,
Doesn't mean we have to listen.
CORPORAL She's got more than the rest of us.
ANDRÉS She thinks she can buy her way into our game?
GILA I'd pull your coins from the table
If they weren't covered by
Your cheap, ugly, sweaty palms.
ANDRÉS Thank you for the kind remark.
May I give your dainty hands a kiss?
How they'd like a stroke from these claws?

GILA Pues conmigo se las corta,
so soldado. ¿No bastaba
para conocer mi humor
lo que no ha muchas semanas
que a los dos pasó conmigo?
ANDRÉS Mírelo bien, sora honrada.
GILA ¿No es él a quien yo molí
a espaldarazos que habla?
¿Tiene más que haber dejado
por los frascos, las reatas,
por el arcabuz, las mulas,
y las ruedas por las cajas?
ANDRÉS Quien lo imaginare digo,
que si no miente, se engaña.
GILA Para tales ocasiones
guardo yo estas bofetadas.

(Dale una bofetada.)

ANDRÉS ¡Las muelas me ha echado fuera!

(Quítase la honda GILA.)

GILA ¡Piedras, Madalena, y salgan
los gallinas, porque acaben
de conocer la Serrana!
CABO ¡Vuacé se tenga, y ninguno
se mueva a sacar la espada,
porque es mujer, en efeto,
y es este cuerpo de guardia!
ANDRÉS Basta que voacé lo diga.
CABO Nunca una mujer agravia.
GERÓNIMO Así lo entiendo.
CABO Pues, sean
amigos.
GILA ¿No dicen nada?
CABO Sus amigos quieren ser.
Déme aquesa mano y basta,
reina.
GILA Yo no soy amiga
de gallinas.

GILA I'd like your cut your nails down to size.
Don't tell me you don't recognize
My pleasant visage, soldier sir?
It was only a few weeks ago
We spent some time together.
ANDRÉS Watch where you're going, good lady.
GILA Isn't he the one whose back
I whipped into quivering cream?
Isn't he the man whose mules
Buckled under the lightest load?
Whose oxen couldn't pull the cart?
Whose wheels went flying off the wagon?
ANDRÉS Anyone who says so is a liar.
GILA I save my blows for moments like these.

(She punches him.)

ANDRÉS What the hell happened to my teeth?!

(Gila takes out her slingshot.)

GILA Get out your stones, Madalena!
We'll send these chickens flying.
They've met their match with La Serrana.
CORPORAL Calm down, fellow. Let no swords be drawn:
After all, she is a woman,
And we are the company guard.
ANDRÉS Yes, fellow. Whatever you say.
CORPORAL Never ever offend a woman.
GERÓNIMO I understand.
CORPORAL Now let's be friends.
GILA They have nothing more to say?
CORPORAL Don't you see, they want to be your friend?
Give me that lovely hand of yours,
And enough of this, my queen.
GILA I'm no friend of any chicken.

Vanse GILA y MADALENA, volviendo GILA la cara.

CABO ¡Mujer brava!
Esta debe ser, sin duda,
la que tiene tanta fama.
ANDRÉS ¡Preguntádselo a mis muelas!
¡No más burlas con serranas!

Vanse.

La REINA DOÑA ISABEL, y el MAESTRE DE CALATRAVA, con ferreruelo de bayeta.

ISABEL Seáis, Maestre, bienvenido.
DON RODRIGO Deme
Vuestra Alteza su mano, que ya he dado
el pésame del Príncipe a su Alteza,
que justamente…
ISABEL ¿Cómo queda Alhama?
DON RODRIGO Ya lo sabréis de boca de la Fama,
que esa fue la ocasión de haber venido
a mostrar la tristeza, que las deudas
de mis obligaciones justamente
publican y en el suelo castellano…
ISABEL ¿Cómo dejáis al Conde, vuestro hermano?
DON RODRIGO Bueno, señora, y de la misma suerte
que yo, lleno del justo sentimiento
de Archidona y Morón, donde ha mostrado
que a tal falta se debe en las fronteras,
que al Príncipe…
ISABEL Es el Conde un gran soldado.
DON RODRIGO Los mal logrados años de su Alteza
son de igual sentimiento con la falta
que tienen estos reinos de heredero,
y más, tan valeroso y tan amable…
ISABEL Maestre, guárdeos Dios.

Exit Gila and Madalena, Gila looking back.

CORPORAL That's one tough woman! Is she
The one we've heard so much about?
ANDRÉS Go ahead and ask my molars!
No more mocking a serrana.

They exit.

[Act Two, Scene 3. Salamanca.]

Queen Isabella and the Master of Calatrava, in a long woolen ecclesiastical cape.

ISABELLA Welcome to you, Master.[82]
DON RODRIGO Give me your hands.
I have just offered His Majesty my
Most sincerest condolences for the Prince,
And fittingly of course…
ISABELLA How fares Alhama?
DON RODRIGO The important news will shortly reach you.
I've merely come to show my tremendous grief,
And so fulfill these debts of obligation
Here on our beloved Castilian soil…
ISABELLA How did you leave your brother, the Count of Ureña?[83]
DON RODRIGO He was fine, señora – that is to say,
Suffering this same sad fate as I,
And full of understandable regret
Because he cannot come pay his respects.
I left him, lamenting the loss of our great Prince,
Somewhere between Archidona and Morón
In our campaign against the heathen Moors…[84]
ISABELLA The Count is a great soldier.
DON RODRIGO The ill fate that
Follows you throughout your years, Your Highness,
Is matched by the unhappy circumstance
That our kingdom now lacks a male heir –
And the one we lost, so kind, so valiant…
ISABELLA May God protect you always, good Master.

Éntrese la REINA, y quede solo el MAESTRE.

DON RODRIGO ¡Valor notable!
No pudo resistir el llanto y quiso
entrarse porque nadie decir pueda
que la ha visto llorar. ¡Oh, castellana
Evadnes! ¡Oh, Semíramis cristiana!
¡Oh, invencible católica española,
tú puedes ser del mundo Fenis sola!

Entre el REY leyendo una carta.

FERNANDO Maestre, ¿adónde está la Reina?
DON RODRIGO Agora
se retiró con sus Altezas.
FERNANDO Basta,
que el rey chico me escribe, deseoso
de hacer paces conmigo y alïanza,
que otra vez a Granada ponga sitio,
porque, como sabéis, están en bandos
él y Muley, su tío, el que posee
la parte de la Alhambra. ¿A quién, Maestre,
a vuestro parecer, podré encargalle
esta ocasión? Porque el marqués de Cádiz,
el señor de Aguilar, el Guzmán Bueno
de Niebla, el gran Ribera, adelantado
de Andalucía, y vuestro hermano el Conde,
y el de Palma se ofrecen a la impresa,
ya que tengo jurada a la Princesa.
DON RODRIGO Pues me llegáis a pedir
parecer, os lo he de dar,
que no tengo de engañar
a quien tengo de servir,
y a hablar verdades me obliga,
después de Isabel y vos,
¡por vida de ambos a dos!,
o el mismo moro lo diga
que en mis vitorias me alaba,
que toca aquesta ocasión
a don Rodrigo Girón,

The Queen exits, and the Master is left alone.

DON RODRIGO What extraordinary courage and strength!
She found herself overcome by grief, and so
Left the room before she burst into tears
So no one could say they saw her weeping.
O fierce Evadne of latter-day Castile!
O Semiramis of our Christian age![85]
O sovereign, invincible Spanish monarch!
Wondrous phoenix of the endless earth!

Enter the King, reading a letter.

FERDINAND Where did the Queen go?
DON RODRIGO She retired
To Your Highness's chambers.
FERDINAND All right.
The Boy King[86] writes me, entreating peace and
An alliance to lay siege to Granada.
He and his uncle, the Sultan Muley Hassan,
Who rules the Alhambra, are in factions.
To whom can I entrust this vital mission?
What about Aguilar, the Marquis of Cádiz?
Guzmán the Good, the one from Niebla?
Or Ribera, High Commander of Andalusia?
What of the Count of Palma? He is able.
There is also, of course, your brother.
All these men offer themselves to this mission,
Which I have sworn to the Infanta to fulfill.[87]
DON RODRIGO Since you asked for my opinion,[88]
I shall honestly give it.
I cannot deceive the monarchs I serve:
I am obliged to speak the truth
To both Isabella and you.
Any Moor will lavish praise
Upon my many victories,
Which bear witness to the mettle
Of the Master of Calatrava,
The great Don Rodrigo Girón.

maestre de Calatrava.
Bien me pueden perdonar
el de Cádiz y el de Niebla,
que el mar de despojos puebla
el de Palma y Aguilar,
el famoso adelantado
que hartos triunfos enseña,
mi hermano, el conde de Ureña,
que esta impresa han deseado,
que son, como he visto yo,
entre desnudos aceros
generosos caballeros,
pero más valientes no.
Y por la cruz que estos pechos
marca, que habéis de mirar
en breve tiempo juntar
a estos dichos muchos hechos.
Los pendones castellanos
marchen a Granada, pues,
que yo os la pondré a los pies
o me cortaré las manos.

FERNANDO Dadme los brazos, Maestre,
que esto fue, a decir verdad,
probar vuestra voluntad.

DON RODRIGO Mi propia sangre la muestre
tantas veces derramada.

FERNANDO No me tenéis que advertir.
Lo que importa es prevenir
brevemente la jornada,
que importa la diligencia
y el hallarme yo presente,
bajando primeramente
por Guadalupe a Plasencia,
a dar a unos bandos fin
que hay entre Carvajales
y Estúñigas.

DON RODRIGO Las reales
presencias, señor, al fin

May those men from Cádiz
And Niebla beg my pardon –
They could truly fill an ocean
With their spoils and their plunder.
The same goes for the High Commander,
And the able Count of Palma:
They all have triumphs of which to boast,
The same is true, I am certain,
Of the noble Count of Ureña,
Who, as you note, is my brother.
Yes, all these men hold nothing back
When asked to flash their steel in battle.
But are they braver men than I? No.
By the cross that marks this breast,
I swear you'll shortly see great deeds
Testifying in bloody battle
To these words I dare to speak.
Let our great Castilian banner
March directly to Granada! –
I'll lay that kingdom at your feet
Or cut off both these hands.

FERDINAND Give me your arms, great Master.
To be truthful, this all was
My way of testing your desire.

DON RODRIGO My blood, spilled in many battles,
Amply shows you that desire.

FERDINAND You need not point it out to me.
What matters now is to prepare
Quickly for this new campaign,
For time is of the essence.
I now need to show my presence:
I'm going to Plasencia
By way of Guadalupe to
Put an end to the enmity
Between the Carvajales and
Their rivals, the Estúñigas.[89]

DON RODRIGO The royal presence unfailingly

acaban cualquiera impresa
con más prisa y brevedad.
FERNANDO Maestre, a besar entrad
las manos a la Princesa.

Éntrense.
El SARGENTO y DON GARCÍA.

SARGENTO Señor Alférez, ya está
en orden la compañía
para marchar.
DON GARCÍA No querría
que se arrepintiese ya
si la moza le ha agradado,
como suele suceder,
porque no llegase a ser
de veras lo imaginado
de burlas.
SARGENTO Con la ocasión
de acercarse el casamiento
debió de cumplir su intento,
que su altiva condición
no pienso que de otra suerte
pudiera nadie rendir.
DON GARCÍA Y aun así ha sido esculpir
un diamante.
SARGENTO ¡Mujer fuerte!
DON GARCÍA Esta noche es la primera
que rindió su voluntad.
SARGENTO Pues si va a decir verdad,
ya amanece. No quisiera
que nos cogiera aquí el día,
porque es, según se me alcanza,
cierta señal de mudanza.
DON GARCÍA Gente viene.

Salga DON LUCAS, el CAPITÁN

CAPITÁN ¿Es don García?
DON GARCÍA Y el sargento.

Brings every undertaking to
Swift and complete success.
FERDINAND Master, let us go and kiss
The hands of the dear Infanta.

They exit.

[Act Two, Scene 4. Garganta la Olla.]

The sergeant and Don García

SERGEANT The company is ready to march.
DON GARCÍA I hope he's not getting regrets
Because he's starting to like the girl.
That kind of thing happens a lot.
God forbid something heartfelt
Comes out of this little joke.
SERGEANT Their wedding day's approaching:
I'm sure he got what he wanted.
How else could have gotten her
To surrender her special prize?
You know how arrogant she is.
DON GARCÍA Easier to mold a diamond.
SERGEANT A strong woman, that's for sure!
DON GARCÍA Tonight's the first night she'll have ever
Given herself over.
SERGEANT First daybreak,
Lieutenant, to be precise.
Let's not get caught here in daylight or
It'll be clear as dawn we're leaving.
DON GARCÍA Someone's coming.

Enter Don Lucas, the captain.

CAPTAIN Don García?
DON GARCÍA And the sergeant.

CAPITÁN Vamos, pues,
que ya cogió la venganza
lo que sembró mi esperanza,
y lo que Gila después,
despierta, habrá de llorar.
DON GARCÍA ¡Buena moza!
CAPITÁN Yo me fundo
en que no la tiene el mundo
en llegándola a gozar.
DON GARCÍA ¡Qué presto que el freno tascas!
CAPITÁN Con la que amor más estima,
en descubriendo el enima
todo es bochorno y bascas.
DON GARCÍA Reniega tú de picarte
y de hallar alguna cosa,
aun en la que no es hermosa,
que pueda cuidado darte
del no sé qué que se dice
que se alcanza por ventura,
que querrás que su hermosura
todo el mundo solenice,
y en los aires andarás,
que también con más rigor
suele ser mosca el amor.
CAPITÁN No me sucedió jamás.
DON GARCÍA A mí sí.
CAPITÁN Vamos de aquí,
y agradézcame el lugar
que no le abraso.
SARGENTO ¡Marchar!
CAPITÁN Yo llegué, engañé y vencí.

Éntrense y toca el atambor a marchar, de adentro dice GILA, y salga luego con un manteo como que se levanta de la cama:

GILA ¡Traición, traición! ¡Padre! ¡Prima!
¡Mingo! ¡Pascual! ¡Antón! ¡Presto,
socorred mi afrenta todos!

CAPTAIN Let's get going.
Revenge just richly harvested
What my dreams and desires sowed.
When Gila wakes, she'll be weeping.
DON GARCÍA Good girl!
CAPTAIN This I know above all:
No one else has ever enjoyed
What I myself just enjoyed.
DON GARCÍA You nibbled on her grass pretty quickly!
CAPTAIN When you're with a girl who believes in love,
It's easy to untie its knot:
The riddle gets solved in a torrent
Of moaning and passion and tears.
DON GARCÍA Don't get bitten by that flea.
Even if the girl's not pretty,
She can make you lose your sleep.
Yes, whoever said it was right:
One prick is all that it takes.
Pretty soon your head's in the clouds
And you're wanting all your buddies
To extol her god-like beauty.
Yes, love's a nasty little bee
That can set you buzzing in circles.
CAPTAIN That has never happened to me.
DON GARCÍA Well, to me, it has.
CAPTAIN Let's go.
And may this little town express
Its gratitude because I repressed
My desire to burn it down.
SERGEANT Let's march!
CAPTAIN I came. I lied. I conquered.

They exit. The sound of marching drum sounds. From offstage, we hear Gila, who immediately enters in petticoats as if she's straight out of bed.

GILA Betrayal! Betrayal! Father![90]
Cousin! Mingo! Pascual! Antón!
Come quickly! My affront
Demands immediate action!

¡Ah de mi casa! ¡Ah del pueblo,
que se me van con mi honor!
¡Que un ingrato caballero
me lleva el alma! ¡Socorro,
que me abraso, que me quemo!
¡Ay, confusos atambores,
enemigos istrumentos
de la muerte y de la envidia,
que en el alma dais los ecos
del ánimo y la venganza,
despertadores soberbios,
relojes de mis desdichas,
de mi agravio pregoneros!,
¿qué os hizo mi honor que vais
tocando al arma y huyendo?
¿Por qué, si vais vitoriosos,
las espaldas habéis vuelto?
¡Esperad, o no venzáis,
que no es bien, cobardes siendo,
dejéis a mi amor vencido
en la muralla del sueño!
¡Ay, furia! ¡Ay, rabia! ¡Ay, cielos,
que se me abrasa el alma! ¡Huego, huego!

Salgan agora alborotados, MADALENA, GIRALDO, PASCUAL y MINGO, envuelto en la manta de la cama.

GIRALDO ¿Qué voces son estas, Gila?
MADALENA Prima, ¿qué es esto?
MINGO ¿Qué es esto?
GILA ¡Mi desdicha y vuestra culpa,
mi engaño y vuestros consejos!
¡Nunca yo diera la mano
por vos a aquel mostro fiero
que en mi afrenta se ha cebado
en mis agravios sangriento,
que no sé, por ella, al alma,
padre, qué invisible huego
me penetró los sentidos

My house! My town! I lose them both
When I lose my honor! Help!
An ungrateful man has taken my heart!
I blaze! I burn! Maddening drums,
You are now my adversaries;
Instruments of death and envy,
Echoing my inner fury,
Summoning my angry spirit,
Sounding out the call to vengeance;
Each beat, the ticking of a clock
Marking my misfortune and
Proclaiming to the entire world
The bitterness of my affront.
What did my honor do to you
That, called to arms, you flee so soon?
If this is your march to victory,
Why do you turn your back on me?
Come back! Return! About face!
This is how you mean to vanquish?
Vanquishing my honor by
Scaling the ramparts of sleep?
O Fury! O Rage! O Heaven!
My heart is in flames! Fire!

Giraldo, Pascual, Madalena enter, disturbed; and Mingo, wrapped in a blanket.

GIRALDO What's all this crying out, Gila?
MADALENA Cousin, what's going on?
MINGO What is it?
GILA My misfortune and your mistake.
My deception and your advice.
I would never have given my hand
To that ferocious monster who
Fattened himself on my affront
If not for you, father. Never.
The fury – I don't know – father –
My heart – the invisible fire –
All my senses have melted

desde la suya de hielo,
qué hechizo me adormeció,
que comencé desde luego
a dársela por los ojos
en amorosos deseos!
¡Reniegue el que es menos sabio
de la de más huerte pecho,
que no hay mujer que resista
en mirando y en oyendo!
Como imaginé que estaba
tan cercano el casamiento,
le di esta noche en mis brazos
ocasión para ofenderos.
¡Mal haya, padre, quien fía
de sus mismos pensamientos,
de palabras de los hombres,
de regalos y requiebros!,
que estas galas enemigas
dicen, tremolando al viento:
«Aquí se alojan agravios
a costa del propio dueño.»
Echaldo de ver, pues marcha
ese capitán Vireno,
haciéndome Olimpia a mí,
y roca su ingrato pecho.
¡Ay, furia! ¡Ay, rabia! ¡Ay, cielos,
que se me abrasa el alma! ¡Huego, huego!

GIRALDO
Las quejas dejemos, Gila,
y acudamos al remedio.

GILA
Bien decís. Dadme un caballo
que imite a mis pensamientos.
Y tú, Madalena, dame
de vestir. Tú, Pascual, luego
dos escopetas me carga.
Tú, Mingo, convoca al pueblo

In his heart of coldest ice.
What evil spell, what black magic,
Made me slumber, made me give myself
To him in amorous desire –
His eyes worked that witchcraft.
The stupidest man in the entire world
Must know no woman can resist
What she sees and what she hears,
No matter how strong her heart.
I thought our wedding day was near,
So gave myself to him last night,
With open arms, and in so doing
Opened you up to this grave offense.
Cursed be the woman who
Dares to trust in her own instincts!
Cursed be she who dares believe
The words of men! Who accepts their gifts!
Who lets herself be swayed and wooed
By their tender little sayings!
These are enemy offerings,
Insubstantial tokens that
Scatter in the slightest wind.
May they declare to the entire world:
'Beware! You will pay our price.'
Go! Take a look. You will see our
Captain Bireno sailing away,
His heart, an ungrateful stone,
As he leaves his Olinpia behind,
Stranded on her desert island.[91]
O Fury! O Rage! O Heaven!
My heart is in flames. Fire!

GIRALDO Enough of this complaining.
Let's see how we can resolve this.

GILA A good idea. Give me a horse,
One that's swift as my racing thoughts.
Madalena, find me some clothes.
Pascual, load me two rifles.
Mingo, gather everyone

para que salgan a darme
ayuda. Y ruego a los cielos
que, ofendidos, no castiguen
a mi enemigo primero,
ni que primero que yo
ninguno le mate, siendo
restaurador de mi honra,
que por estos brazos mesmos
mi agravio quiero vengar,
que solo a todos les ruego
que vengan a ser testigos
de la suerte que me vengo.
Y guárdense de mí todos
cuantos hombres tiene el suelo
si a mi enemigo no alcanzo,
que hasta matarlo no pienso
dejar hombre con la vida.
Y hago al Cielo juramento
de no volver a poblado,
de no peinarme el cabello,
de no dormir desarmada,
de comer siempre en el suelo
sin manteles, y de andar
siempre al agua, al sol y al viento
sin que me acobarde el día
y sin que me venza el sueño,
y de no alzar, finalmente,
los ojos a ver el cielo
hasta morir o vengarme.

MINGO ¡Todos decimos lo mesmo!

GIRALDO ¡Ea! ¿A qué esperamos, hija?
Vamos de aquí.

GILA ¡Rabio y muero!
¡Sin honra estoy! ¡Vamos, padre,
que de coraje reviento!

In town to come to my aid.
And God help me, let no one
Punish him before I can.
Yes, no one else must kill him.
I alone must restore my honor,
Myself, with my own two arms.
I only ask you to bear witness
To my act of revenge and
Keep me away from every man
On this wide earth, for if I fail
To find this enemy of mine,
I swear by holy heaven above,
I will leave no man alive
I will never return to any town,
Never brush my hair again and
Never go to sleep unarmed.
I'll eat my food upon bare ground.
I'll wander forever through driving rain
And blowing wind and burning sun,
My eyes wide open to the day
Every single waking minute,
And when night falls, I will never
Close them for a moment's sleep.
I will never lift those eyes
To the skies again until
I die or I am avenged.

MINGO We all say exactly the same thing!

GIRALDO What are we waiting for? Let's go!

GILA I rage, I die. I have no honor,
I explode with passion and anger.

¡Ay, furia! ¡Ay, rabia! ¡Ay, cielos,
que se me abrasa el alma! ¡Huego! ¡Huego!

FIN DEL ACTO SEGUNDO

Jesús María Josef
Luis Úrsola Francisco Juan Antonio

O Fury! O Rage! O Heaven!
My heart is in flames! Fire!

END OF ACT TWO.

Jesús María Josef
Luis Úrsola Francisco Juan Antonio[92]

ACTO TERCERO

De adentro VOCES.

¡Echa! ¡Hao, a man derecha
por el camino de abajo!

Sale MINGO.

MINGO No hay atajo sin trabajo.
Cualquiera senda es estrecha.
Temeroso de encontrar
con Gila, que airada y huerte,
como si huera la muerte,
nadie quiere perdonar,
que como en el Capitán
su agravio no santisfizo,
y el juramento que hizo
en cuantos vienen y van
cumpre valerosamente,
siendo tan brava homecida,
que no deja con la vida
padre, amigo ni pariente.
Por aquesa cordillera
me arrojé con un rocín
que está cerca de su fin.
¡Nunca yo se lo pidiera
al boticario emprestado!
Que no sé en esta ocasión
qué muermo le dio, o torzón,
que dio conmigo en el prado
y no hay remedio con él
de podelle levantar.
Bueno volveré al lugar
con esta nueva y sin él.
Para de aquí a Jarandilla
a pata pudiera ir yo.
¿Quién, dïabros, me subió
desde ell albarda a la silla?

ACT THREE

[Act Three, Scene 1. In the sierra.]

Offstage voices.

VOICES *(off)* Down that way! To the right!
Careful now! Take the low road!

Enter Mingo.

MINGO It's hard work, taking the easy way.
Every short cut is straight and narrow.
I'm scared I'll come across Gila.
She's raging, on the rampage.
Like death, she pardons no one.
The Captain's act remains unavenged,
And so she faithfully fulfills her oath
With every man she comes across –
She is one tough murderess!
And there's no friend or relation
Whose life she'd deign to spare,
Not even her own father.
As for me, I've come flying
Down the sierra on a workhorse,
Stumbling along on his last legs.
I never should have borrowed him
From that damn apothecary!
I don't know what fever hit him
Up there on the high plateau,
But there's no getting the beast
Back on his own four feet.
The best I can do is head for home:
I can get to Xarandilla
On my own two hooves.
What damn devil persuaded me
To saddle up in that sad saddle?

¡Ojo, que tendido está!
No hay esperanza tan larga.
Él se arrojó con la carga.
Quiero volver, y quizá
que se levante ser puede,
asiéndole por la cola,
pero temo que ella sola
en la mano se me quede,
según está desmayado
y tien la cola madura.
Yo tengo poca ventura.
¡Nunca más rocín prestado!

Éntrese, y comience UNO a cantar este romance desde adentro:

CAMINANTE *Allá en Garganta la Olla,*
en la Vera de Plasencia,
salteóme una serrana,
blanca, rubia, ojimorena.
Botín argentado calza,
media pajiza de seda,
alta basquiña de grana
que descubre media pierna.
Sobre cuerpos de palmilla
suelto airosamente lleva
un capote de dos faldas
hecho de la misma mezcla.

Agora vaya bajando por la sierra abajo, abriendo una cabaña que estará hecha arriba GILA LA SERRANA, como la pinta el romance, sin hablar.

El cabello sobre el hombro
lleva partido en dos crenchas,
y una montera redonda
de plumas blancas y negras.
De una pretina dorada
dorados frascos le cuelgan
al lado isquierdo un cuchillo,
y en el hombro una escopeta.

Look! He's flat out on the ground,
Subscribing to that timeless adage:
'Hurry up and wait.' And my load –
He's dropped it on the ground!
If I shake him by the tail,
Maybe he'll jump up to his feet,
Though probably I'll end up with
Just the tail, a rotten apple
Plucked from a dying tree.
I am totally out of luck.
To hell with rented workhorses!

He exits. Offstage, a man's voice is heard singing this ballad:

TRAVELER *(off)* Once in Garganta la Olla,
In La Vera of Plasencia,
I was assaulted by a serrana
With darkest eyes and lightest hair.
Her boots, they sparkled with silver,
Her stockings were soft as silk,
Her skirts, all colored in scarlet,
Revealed more than half of a leg.
Her clothes were made of blue linen,
And she had a marvelous cloak
Folded over in two places,
Made of blue linen the same.

Gila comes out of her cabin and starts making her way down the sierra, not speaking. She is just as the ballad describes her.

TRAVELER [off] Her hair, flowing down to her shoulders,
Is parted right down the middle,
With a rounded cap above it,
Plumed with black and white feathers.
A gilded belt girdles her figure,
Cinched firmly around her slim waist.
From it, a powder box dangles,
Golden ties hold it tightly in place.
On her left side, she has a hunting knife,
And over her shoulder, a rifle.

Si saltea con las armas,
también con ojos saltea.

(Pone agora la escopeta entre las ramas, y dice:)

GILA ¡Tente, caminante!
CAMINANTE ¡Ay, Dios!
GILA ¡Apéate! ¡Acaba!
CAMINANTE ¡Espera!
(*Ap.:* ¡Que hobe de encontralla aquí
pensando que era conseja!)
GILA ¿Dónde vienes?
CAMINANTE De Toledo.
GILA ¿Adónde vas?
CAMINANTE A Plasencia.
GILA ¿Qué dinero llevas?
CAMINANTE Poco.
GILA Saca luego cuanto llevas.
CAMINANTE En esta bolsa va todo.
Perdona el ser poco.
GILA Muestra.
Tú cantas mal y porfías.
CAMINANTE Tu historia pienso que es esta.
GILA Ya sé que es mi historia.
CAMINANTE Agora
no solamente en la Vera,
sino en Castilla, no cantan
otra cosa, y tu belleza
a tu fama se aventaja.
GILA ¿Parézcote hermosa?
CAMINANTE Afrentas
al sol, al alba, a las flores.
GILA ¿Estimaras que te hiciera
favor?
CAMINANTE Y será bien grande
si con la vida me dejas.
GILA Esa sierra arriba sube,
que en la cumbre de esa sierra
tengo una choza en que vivo,

She assaults men with her arms
And she assaults them with her eyes.

[Enter the Traveler.[93]]
She points the rifle at him through some branches, and says:

GILA Stop right there, traveler.
TRAVELER God help me!
GILA Enough of this! On your feet!
TRAVELER Please, wait.
(aside) This must be her.
And I thought it was all just legend!
GILA Where are you coming from?
TRAVELER Toledo.
GILA Where are you headed?
TRAVELER Plasencia.
GILA How much money do you have on you?
TRAVELER Not much.
GILA Show me what you've got.
TRAVELER Everything I have is in this bag.
Pardon – It's not much.
GILA Show it to me!
By the way: you sing badly.
TRAVELER I was simply singing your story.
GILA Don't tell me about my story.
TRAVELER Everyone is singing about you,
Not just here in La Vera,
But throughout all Castile.
If I may say so, your beauty
Far outshines your reputation.
GILA Do I seem beautiful to you?
TRAVELER You shame the sun, the dawn, the flowers.
GILA You think you're worthy of my favor?
TRAVELER The worthiest favor would be
To let me go on living.
GILA That sierra you see goes up and up,
And at the top of the highest ridge,
There's a cabin of oaken timbers:

de encinas y robles hecha,
donde quiero que conmigo
hasta ver el alba duermas,
que desde allí con el día
podrás pasar a Plasencia.

CAMINANTE ¡Tuyo soy! ¡Daréte el alma!

GILA Sube.

CAMINANTE ¿Qué cruces son estas?

GILA De hombres que he muerto.

CAMINANTE Desdicen
tu hermosura y tu fiereza.

GILA Tengo razón de mostralla.

CAMINANTE ¡Qué altas están estas peñas!

GILA Pues desde aquí has de ir al río.

(Arrójale.)

CAMINANTE ¡Engañásteme, sirena!

GILA También a mí me engañaron.

(Pone una cruz que estará hecha de dos palos pequeños.)

Esta cruz te debo. Tenga
el Cielo de ti piedad.
Gente parece que suena.
Otro cayó en el garlito.
No es hombre. Parece bestia,
aunque camina en dos pies,
con silla y freno.

Entre MINGO, con la silla puesta y apretadas las cinchas, y el freno puesto en la cabeza también.

MINGO ¡Que venga
de esta suerte un hombre humano
por llevar cosas ajenas!
En sus trece dio el rocín,
que esto de dar de cabeza
porfïando en una cosa
es de necios y de bestias.
Bien es verdad que acabó

It's where I live.[94] I want you
To sleep beside me there tonight.
You can continue on your way
To Plasencia at dawn.

TRAVELER I am yours. I'll give you my heart!

GILA Start climbing.

TRAVELER What are these crosses for?

GILA Men I've killed.

TRAVELER This fierceness contradicts your beauty.

GILA I have my reasons.

TRAVELER This hill is steep!

GILA Yes, but from here the way is easy:
You dive straight down to the river.

TRAVELER You deceived me, serrana!

(She throws him off the cliff.)

GILA Just as I once was deceived.

She puts up a cross, made of two small sticks.

GILA I owe you the debt of this cross.
May heaven take pity on you.
Someone seems to be coming:
Another man falls in my snare,
Though this one strangely appears
More like a mule than a man.

Enter Mingo wearing the saddle and horse gear, with the reins draped over his head.

MINGO Is this fit for a human being?
Saddled up and saddled down?
[Because the workhorse was hard-headed,
Now I'm feeling double leaded,
And this load is hard on my head as well.
He was stubborn like a mule,
But then he took off like a bird

como si un pájaro huera.
Todos hemos de parar
en esto mismo por huerza.
¡Oh, necesidad infame,
que a un hombre ensillas y enfrenas!
Pero quien merece albarda,
no es mucho que silla tenga.
¡Pardiobre, yo di con Gila!
¿Qué he de her? ¡Mas linda treta
me ofrece el freno y la silla,
que me matará esta fiera
en sabiendo que soy hombre!
Hoy me ha de valer ser bestia.
Yo me pongo en cuatro pies
y tiro coces soberbias,
y doy saltos y relincho,
y piso y hago corvetas.

GILA Este villano procura
engañarme, y por la mesma
treta cogerle imagino.

MINGO ¡Ciégala, Santa Guiteria!

GILA Caballito, caballito,
el de las piernas de jerga,
por la virtud que hay en ti
que me digas quién te lleva,

(MINGO pónese en dos pies.)

quién te rige, quién te manda,
quién te da cebada nueva,
quién te enfrena, quién te ensilla,
quién te limpia, quién te hierra.

MINGO ¡Por la gracia de Dios Padre
el caballo hablado hobiera
las palabras que decía!
Eran en su misma lengua.
Mingo soy, que ando perdido
hoy en fegura de bestia,
aunque el mismo papel hacen
muchos vestidos de seda.

And flew up straight to heaven.
Well, we're all headed there anyhow.
Reined in by my very own reins,
Misery my only spur! –
But as they say, if you want to travel,
You can't do it without a saddle.][95]
Word of God! I've come across Gila!
How do I slip out of this?
This saddle offers a pretty trick.
If she finds out I'm a man,
That beast will be the end of me,
So I'll be the beast, on all fours,
And stamp like crazy and jump and buck
And crook my legs and kick up dust.

GILA This peasant wants to deceive me.
Well, two can play at that game.

MINGO O Holy Saint Quiteria,
Patron saint of myopia,
Close her eyes and work your wonders![96]

GILA Horsey, horsey, little horsey,
With your coarse and hairy legs,
If there's any good inside you,
Tell me who is meant to ride you,
Who shall rule you, who shall drive you,
Who shall feed you oats and hay,
Who shall sit upon your saddle
And clean you at the end of day.

(Mingo gets up on two feet.[97])

MINGO For the love of God the Father,
You drive this horse to speak your tongue!
I am Mingo, I am lost,
And, yes, strangely, dressed like a horse,
Though dress a monkey in silk,
He's still the same sad monkey.

Prestóme, por mi desdicha,
o por la suya pudiera
decir mejor, un caballo
para llegarme a esta aldea
allá nuestro boticario,
que según dijo el albéitar
que nació con él, cumplía
cincuenta años estas hierbas,
y diole tan gran torzón
atravesando esta sierra,
que se quedó como espada,
aunque fue espada sin vuelta.
Y ensillado y enfrenado,
como ves de esta manera,
vuelvo a Garganta la Olla.

GILA De tu desdicha me pesa.

MINGO Soy desdichado en rocines.

GILA Nadie es dichoso con bestias.
¿Qué hay nuevo en el lugar,
Mingo?

MINGO Mil cosas hay nuevas.

GILA ¿Vive el cura?

MINGO Y su sobrina
se hue a casar a Plasencia
a un hidalgo.

GILA ¿Y el sastre?

MINGO Murió.

GILA San Dimas le sea
con Dios abogado, Mingo.

MINGO El que heredó las tijeras
hue el sacristán, porque a todos
corta de vestir su lengua,
y ha dado, a pesar del mundo,
en ser músico y poeta.

GILA No hay cosa agora más fácil.

Due to a sad misfortune –
Or should I say, the steed's –
I borrowed something resembling
A horse to get to that hamlet
Way down there in the valley.
Thank God for apothecaries!
Our village veterinarian
Knew better far better than he –
Did I mention he was born
The same day as that youthful horse,
Fifty-some-odd years ago?!
Yes, that horse has been grazing grass
For half a sainted century,
And sick to his stomach he
Vomited across the sierra
Like an arrow, then hit his target,
The cold hard ground, where he's still lodged.
That's why I'm saddled this way,
Bound for Garganta la Olla.

GILA Your misfortune weighs on me.

MINGO It weighs on me too. Like a saddle.

GILA No one's lucky when it comes
To horses. What's new in town,
Mingo?

MINGO A thousand different things.

GILA Is the priest still alive?

MINGO Yes, and
The old man's niece moved to Plasencia
To wed a poor gentleman.

GILA What about the tailor?

MINGO Dead.

GILA May Saint Dismas of the cross
Plead for him before God.[98]

MINGO The sexton inherited his spool and thread,
But there's no sewing up his mouth:
He wants to be a singer and poet,
In spite of what everyone tells him.

GILA So does everyone nowadays

MINGO También compone comedias
tan malas, que dicen todos:
«No las hagas, no las temas.»
GILA ¿Qué se ha hecho el escribano?
MINGO Metido en causas ajenas,
levantando testimoños
y el arancel por guinea.
GILA ¿Murió Pero Grullo?
MINGO Huése
a Jarandilla, y su nuera
con el sacristán de Cuacos,
que es rofián por la igreja.
GILA ¿Y el barbero?
MINGO Tabardillos
con el boticario juega,
y van horros a matar
con el médico y albéitar.
GILA ¿Y el albardero?
MINGO Enviudó
agora por la Cuaresma.
GILA No hay albarda que no mate,
y muchas con mayor fuerza.
MINGO Y quien las merece, más.
GILA ¿Qué se hizo Maricrespa?
MINGO Casóse con Juan Carrasco.
GILA ¿Y mi prima Madalena?
MINGO Agora pienso que trata
de casarse, aunque desea
irse a Plasencia a vivir.
GILA ¡Casen muy enhorabuena!
MINGO No se usa otra cosa ya,
y no hay quien no se arrepienta,
y siempre tienen los curas
que her. No habrá quien lo entienda.
GILA ¿Qué ha hecho Dios de mi padre?
MINGO Tus desdichas y tu afrenta
pesa a lágrimas.
GILA ¡Buen viejo!

MINGO It gets worse: he's also writing plays.
Bad ones. Everyone tells him:
'Have some courage, don't be scared
To give something else a try.'
[GILA What is the notary up to?
MINGO Minding other people's business.
Collecting testimony –
And fees, of course – by the peso.
GILA Did Pero Grullo finally die?
MINGO Worse. He moved to Xarandilla.
His daughter-in-law ran off
With the sexton from Cuacos.
Another fine man of the church.
GILA And the barber?
MINGO Still playing cards
With the apothecary,
Teaming up against the doctor
And the vet.
GILA And the saddle maker?
MINGO Poor man, widowed this past Lent.
GILA Well, a saddle can kill you.
MINGO Especially if you deserve it.
GILA What became of Maricrespa?
MINGO She went and married Juan Carrasco.
GILA And my cousin Madalena?
MINGO I think she's planning to marry too,
And then move to the big city,
Plasencia.
GILA May they enjoy
The happiest of marriages!
MINGO It's what everyone is doing,
And what everyone's regretting.
No one can tell you why they do it,
And the priests just go along.][99]
GILA How has God been treating my father?
MINGO Your misfortunes and the affront
To his honor grieve him to tears.
GILA Kind old man!

MINGO Diéronle casi por huerza
la vara de alcalde agora.
GILA Querrá prenderme con ella.
MINGO Dios te libre, Gila, amén,
de que la Hermandad te prenda,
que a la he, que te despachen,
que la de toda la Vera
anda en tu busca.
GILA   No importa
mientras yo tengo estas peñas
donde vivo por muralla,
y estos brazos por defensa.
MINGO Quinientos escudos dan
a quien traiga tu cabeza.
GILA Escarmentará en la suya
quien no hiciere en la ajena.
MINGO Mira si me mandas más,
que con una silla a cuestas
aun suele aguarse un rocín.
GILA ¿Pues ya, Mingo, no te acuerdas
del juramento que he hecho
hasta que vengue mi ofensa?
MINGO Luego, ¿yo soy de los hombres
que también entran en cuenta
de tu venganza?
GILA   Sí, Mingo.
MINGO ¿No me escusará siquiera
el hábito de rocín?
GILA Si fueras rocín sin lengua,
pudiera ser permitillo,
pero rocín que habla, muera,
que no hay entre los rocines
rocín, por poco que sepa,
que por lo menos tal vez
no tire coces y muerda.
Lo que puedo her por ti,
Mingo, por ser de una tierra
y en una casa crïados,

MINGO They practically had to
Force the Mayor's staff of office
Into his hands.
GILA He'll probably
Use its power to hunt me down.
MINGO May God help you escape the clutches
Of the holy Brotherhood![100]
All its members in La Vera
Mean to catch you, and, God help me,
Bring you to justice.
GILA Who cares.
These crags and cliffs around us
Are ramparts to protect me, and
These arms are ready to defend me.
MINGO They've placed a bounty on your head of
Five hundred escudos.
GILA Let each man
Be his own example before
He makes example of others.
MINGO Anything else you need from me?
This horse is very tired and
Needs to be on his way.
GILA Do you forget what I swore to do
Until my offense was avenged?
MINGO So I'm to be another tally
In your account book of revenge?
GILA Yes, Mingo.
MINGO I don't get some
Special dispensation for
Dressing like a workhorse for you?
GILA If you couldn't talk, perhaps.
But a horse that has a tongue must die.
I have never seen a horse,
No matter how stupid and coarse,
Who wouldn't bite his master.
What I can do for you, Mingo,
Since we were born and raised
On the same land, in the same house,

es que escojas la manera
de muerte que más gustares.

MINGO (*Ap.:* ¡Miren qué paño o qué seda
para que corte un vestido!

GILA Y esto ha de ser muy apriesa,
que tengo donde acudir,
y he sabido que a Plasencia
van los Reyes, y querría
ver si va gente de guerra
con ellos, que puede acaso
ir mi enemigo, y mi ofensa
satisfacer como aguardo,
ya que mi contraria estrella
quiso que errase el camino
cuando le seguí. ¿Qué esperas?

MINGO No más de saber de ti
en qué tantos grados era
tu pariente este rocín,
que con mi muerte le vengas.

GILA No estoy, Mingo, para burlas.

MINGO Luego, ¿díceslo de veras?

GILA Presto lo verás.

(De adentro.)

¡Ataja!
¡Al agua, al agua!

GILA Esta es fiera
que algunos monteros siguen.
Del Rey son, porque esta sierra,
de miedo que en ella vivo,
los cazadores respetan.
Mingo, para darte espacio
que tu muerte escoger puedas,
atado quiero dejarte
de un robre hasta dar la vuelta.
Muestra las manos, que aquí
traigo guardada una cuerda,
con que algunos hombres ato
para echarlos de estas peñas.

Is let you choose the manner
Of your death.[101]

MINGO *(aside)* Wonderful.
Like picking out cloth for a dress!

GILA Just do it quickly, Mingo.
I have somewhere I need to be.
The King and Queen are bound for Plasencia:
I want to see which troops are with them.
My enemy may be lurking there,
Maybe I can take my revenge,
Maybe I can overcome
The malicious star in heaven above
That caused me to lose track of him
The very first night of the hunt.
What are you hoping for right now?

MINGO To never see you again.
Take your revenge on this workhorse
Who was once your close relation.

GILA Don't mock me, Mingo.

MINGO So you mean
To do what you say?

GILA You'll soon see.

(Offstage voice.)

VOICE (off) Cut him off! Down to the water!

GILA Some men pursuing a beast.
These huntsmen must be the King's:
Local hunters, for fear of me,
Stay clear of this sierra.
Take this time to choose your death.
I'm tying you to this oak
Until I'm back. Give me your hands.
This is my rope for tying men up
Before I hurl them off this cliff.

(Átale de un roble.)

MINGO — Como me ves ensillado
y en este prado me dejas,
trabas me quieres echar.
¿Quién vio tan grande fiereza?

GILA — Yo daré la vuelta, Mingo,
tan presto que te arrepientas.

(De adentro.)

¡Al arroyo! ¡Ataja, ataja!

GILA — ¡Por aquí las voces suenan!

Éntrese GILA, y diga MINGO, atado al roble:

MINGO — Los que rocines matáis
que para un camino os prestan,
catad bien la historia mía
porque escarmentéis en ella,
que en el trebunal que rige
la Serrana de la Vera
pide su sangre josticia
contra mi pobre inocencia.

De adentro.

¡Ataja!

OTRO, *dentro.* — Para seguirle
entre las ramas espesas
de ese jaral intricado
dejó el caballo su Alteza.

MINGO — ¡Oh, si viniese algún hombre
que desatarme pudiera!

Entre el REY DON FERNANDO, con un venablo.

FERNANDO — Cebado en el jabalí,
a la falda de esta sierra
he llegado. ¡Oh, caza, imagen
justamente de la guerra,
como de la muerte el sueño!

MINGO — Un hombre he visto entre aquellas

(She ties him to an oak.)

MINGO — Aren't I reined in enough already?
Has such cruelty ever been seen?
GILA — I'll be back so quickly, Mingo,
That you'll be sorry you said that.

(Offstage.)

VOICE (off) — Down to the creek! Cut him off!
GILA — The voices are coming from here.

Gila exits. Mingo, tied to the oak, speaks:

MINGO — Those of you who'd kill a workhorse
That you rented for a journey,
Take good notice of my story,
Let it serve as an example.
In this high court of La Vera
Ruled over by La Serrana,
Justice is served with innocent blood.

Offstage.

VOICE *(off)* — Cut him off!
ANOTHER *(off)* — He dismounted!
His Majesty's chasing the prey
Into that rock rose thicket!
MINGO — If only someone would untie me!

Enter King Ferdinand, with a lance.

FERDINAND — Bent on besting a wild boar,
I've come to the base of this high ridge.
The hunt! How thrilling! Mirror of war,
Just as sleep is mirror of death.
MINGO — I see a man in that thicket,

ramas del jaral. Sin duda
es ángel que Dios ordena
que me venga a desatar.

FERNANDO ¡Qué peñascos! ¡Qué aspereza!
MINGO ¡Hola! ¡Hao, hombre de bien!
FERNANDO Allí un hombre me vocea.
MINGO ¡Hao! ¡A la sierra acá arriba!
FERNANDO Quiero llegarme más cerca.
MINGO Ya viene. Gran dicha ha sido.
FERNANDO Villano es.
MINGO Si escapo de esta,
a la imagen más devota
prometo un Mingo de cera.
FERNANDO Atado, si no me engaño,
a un roble está.
MINGO Pues las muestras
tiene de noble, señor,
mostrad hoy vuestra nobleza
en desatarme de aquí,
si tenéis de mí cremencia.

(Comiéncele a desatar.)

FERNANDO ¿Quién de esta suerte te puso?
MINGO La Serrana de la Vera.
FERNANDO ¿Esa mujer anda aquí?
MINGO No tiene palmo esta sierra,
este bosque ni ese valle
donde no haya una cruz puesta
de los hombres que ella mata,
porque las pone ella mesma.
No sé esta Hermandad que han hecho
los Reyes, para qué es buena,
pues no prende este dïabro
que a todos mata y saltea.
Guárdeos Dios, que me habéis dado
la vida, que estaba puesta
al tabrero de su gusto.

Like an angel sent by heaven
To untie me.

FERDINAND What harsh terrain!
What heights!

MINGO Hallo! Ho! My good man!

FERDINAND Someone calls me.

MINGO Ho! Up here!
Up on the ridge!

FERDINAND I'll approach.

MINGO He's coming! My lucky day!

FERDINAND A lowly peasant.

MINGO If I survive this,
I vow to go to church and bow down
Before the holiest icon
And light a little wax candle for
This Mingo that went un-mangled.

FERDINAND It looks like he's tied to an oak.

MINGO All signs point to your being
A nobleman, señor.
Show your noble manhood, please,
By nobly unknotting me.

(He starts to untie him.)

FERDINAND Who left you tied up like this?

MINGO La Serrana de la Vera.

FERDINAND Is that woman around here?

MINGO You can't find a spot of ground
Anywhere in this sierra,
Whether up here in these woods
Or down there in the valley,
Where she hasn't placed a cross
To mark a man she's murdered.
What good is the Holy Brotherhood,
That royal posse duly dispatched
By the King and Queen themselves,
If it can't apprehend that devil?
God keep you, you've given me life
By getting me out of checkmate.

FERNANDO ¿Cómo te dejó con ella?
MINGO Porque tuvo aviso aquí
que pasa el Rey a Plasencia,
y no sé qué novedades,
juntamente con la Reina,
y piensa que un enemigo
de quien vengarse desea
vendrá con ellos acaso,
y hasta dar, señor, la vuelta,
como veis me deja atado.
Yo me voy, y guardaos de ella,
que es una tíguere.
FERNANDO ¡Aguarda!
¿Cómo vas de esa manera?
MINGO Porque quien mata un rocín
está obligado de esta pena.

Éntrese MINGO, y dicen de adentro:

¡Muera!
FERNANDO ¿Qué es esto?
MAESTRE. ¡Matalda!
GILA ¡Aquí aguardo en estas peñas!
MINGO ¡Y yo en Garganta la Olla!
GILA Aquí aguarda un hombre. ¡Muera!

(Encara la escopeta, y vuelve la cara el REY DON FERNANDO.)

FERNANDO Tente, mujer.
GILA Si la cara
no vuelves, Castilla queda
sin rey, como queda agora
sin príncipe –Que Dios tenga–,
que de ti mismo me dio
luego tu persona nuevas,
si los ojos no me engañan,
de haberte visto en Plasencia,
mas las personas reales

FERDINAND Why didn't she choose to kill you?
MINGO She heard the King was passing through
On his way to Plasencia,
The Queen by his side, etcetera,
And she has it in her mind
Some enemy she hopes to find
May be with them, and so she left me
Tied up here till she's less tied up.
I'm off. Beware of her, señor.
She's a ferocious tiger.
FERDINAND Wait!
You're going on your way like that?
MINGO He who rides a horse to death
Deserves a horse's punishment.

Offstage, they say:

VOICES *(off)* Die!
FERDINAND What's going on?
DON RODRIGO *[off]* Kill her!

[Enter Gila.[102]]

GILA I'll be waiting by this cliff!
MINGO And I, in Garganta la Olla!

Exit Mingo.

GILA Another man? He dies!

She raises the rifle. King Ferdinand turns his face away.

FERDINAND Hold back, woman.
GILA If you refuse to show me your face,
Castile will find itself not merely
Without a Prince, God be with him,
But without a King as well.
[You are your own messenger:
You disclose the King's presence.
I have seen you in Plasencia and][103]
I cannot be deceived.
Royalty may attempt to conceal

tan grande secreto encierran,
que, aun no siendo conocidas,
con el alma se respetan.

FERNANDO El Rey soy, serrana.

GILA ¡Vivas
eternos años, y seas
señor de cuanto ve el sol,
con la que es hermosa hiedra
de tus brazos Isabel,
que, quitada la montera,
te reverencio, Fernando,
por ley de naturaleza,
como a mi rey y señor!

FERNANDO ¿No te he visto yo en Plasencia?

GILA Asir un toro me viste
por los cuernos en las fiestas
que te hicieron, y rendillo.

FERNANDO ¿Y por qué ocasión salteas
dando muerte a cuantos pasan?

GILA Por satisfacer la ofensa
de un hombre, y hasta matalle
he prosupuesto que mueran
con solene juramento
cuantos encontrare, y piensa
que tú solo has sido el hombre
que perdona mi fiereza.
Y no quiebro el juramento,
que el Rey es Dios en la Tierra,
en el lugar suyo. Fernando,
la justicia representas,
y pues no eres hombre, voy
a buscar hombres que puedan
hartar la sed de mi agravio,
que es hidrópica mi afrenta,
y al que mujeres agravia,
castigar.

FERNANDO Serrana bella,
guárdate de mi Hermandad.

Its whereabouts, yet it reveals
Its special grace to respectful souls.

FERDINAND I am the King, serrana.

GILA May you live forever and ever!
And rule everything under the sun! –
Entwined in the lovely ivy of
Your beautiful Isabella.
I take off my hood and bow down.
The law of nature commands respect.
You are my lord – Ferdinand.

FERDINAND Didn't I see you in Plasencia?

GILA You saw me seize a wild bull
And subdue it, at the fiesta.

FERDINAND Why do you assault and murder
Every man who passes by?

GILA To avenge the offense of a man.
I have sworn to kill every man I meet
Until I meet and kill this man.
You alone have quelled my wrath,
You alone have earned my pardon,
And I do not break my solemn vow
Since the King is God on earth,
And represents God's justice,
You are therefore not a man.
I'll go in search of other men
To quench the thirst my affront compels,
Though such a thirst can never be quenched,
No matter how many times one drinks.
Endless are the men on earth
Who have wronged a decent woman,
And in so doing earned themselves
My punishment.

FERDINAND Lovely serrana,
Beware my Holy Brotherhood.

GILA ¡Guárdense de mi escopeta!
¿Un hombre no estaba aquí
atado?
FERNANDO Yo por mis mesmas
manos le corté los lazos.
GILA A tus manos lo agradezca,
que ese también se me escapa.

Entre el MAESTRE DON RODRIGO GIRÓN.

DON RODRIGO ¡Locos nos trae Vuestra Alteza!
FERNANDO Cebéme en el jabalí,
Maestre.
DON RODRIGO Dadme licencia
agora para matar
esa mujer, esa fiera
que ha muerto cuatro monteros
vuestros con esa escopeta.

(Retirándose GILA.)

GILA Maestre de Calatrava,
reportaos, por vida vuestra,
que aún hay dentro munición
y está el gatillo muy cerca.
FERNANDO Dejalda. Vete.
GILA Yo haré
lo que me mandáis, y advierta
Vuestra Alteza que esta vida
me debe más.
FERNANDO Esa es deuda
que yo os la agradezco y todo.
GILA Guarde Dios a vuecelencia.

Vase.

DON RODRIGO ¡Estraña mujer!
FERNANDO ¡Notable!
Vamos a buscar la Reina.
DON RODRIGO Un caballo tengo aquí.

GILA Let them beware my rifle!
Wasn't there a man here, tied up?
FERDINAND I cut him loose with my own hands.
GILA May he show those hands respect,
For he has escaped from me too.

Enter the Master, Don Rodrigo Girón.

DON RODRIGO Your Highness had us deeply worried.
FERDINAND I got lost chasing that wild boar.
DON RODRIGO Give me license to kill that beast,
That woman, who's killed four of
Your huntsmen with her rifle.
GILA Master of Calatrava, be calm:
I still have one bullet left,
And the trigger is poised and ready.
FERDINAND Put aside the rifle aside and be gone.
GILA I will do what you command.
Let your Highness be appraised:
Here is yet another man's life
For which you're indebted to me.
FERDINAND I acknowledge this great debt.
GILA May God keep you from all harm.

She exits.

DON RODRIGO Strange woman!
FERDINAND Remarkable!
Let's go find the Queen.
DON RODRIGO Take this horse.

FERNANDO No será la vez primera
que a sus reyes dan caballos
los Girones.
DON RODRIGO Vuestra Alteza
como quien es sabe honrarnos.
FERNANDO Con grande estremo me lleva,
Maestre, admirado agora
la Serrana de la Vera.

Vanse.

Salgan de camino, con botas y espuelas, DON LUCAS y DON GARCÍA, y ferreruelos puestos.

CAPITÁN Andrés, quita esos frenos a las mulas,
pues el camino hemos perdido y vamos
tan cansados, que luego encontraremos
pastor o caminante que nos ponga
en el real camino de Plasencia.

Entre ANDRÉS con la bota.

ANDRÉS Mientras hay bota, puede haber paciencia.
¡Brindis, señor don Lucas, y rebrindis
al señor don García!
DON GARCÍA Con el agua
de ese arroyuelo la razón haremos,
que convida al sediento y caluroso
en búcaros de juncia bullicioso.
ANDRÉS No dijera un poeta de romances
eso mejor, pintando un verde prado,
y más cuando su dama lo ha pisado.
Sobre la hierba que este nos ofrece
hasta ver si parece alguna guía
reclinemos los cuerpos, don García.
DON GARCÍA Soy de ese parecer.
ANDRÉS Y yo del propio.

(Tiéndese sobre la hierba.)

Sirva lo que he bebido de frezada,
y la señora bota de almohada.

FERDINAND It won't be the first time a Girón
Has lent a horse to the crown.[104]
DON RODRIGO Your Highness has always been a man
Who knows how to do us honor.
FERDINAND I am overwhelmed. Astonished by
La Serrana de la Vera!

They exit.

[Act Three, Scene 2. In the sierra.]

Enter Captain Don Lucas and Don García. They are in traveling clothes and ferreruelos.[105]

CAPTAIN Andrés, loosen up the reins on those mules.[106]
We've lost our way, we're exhausted: let's pray
Some traveler or shepherd shows us
The way back to the high road to Plasencia.

Enter Andrés with a wine skin.

ANDRÉS As long as there's wine, nothing to worry about.
A toast, Don Lucas! And a second toast
To our lieutenant, good old Don García!
DON GARCÍA We can toast with water from this stream.
It invites the parched and thirsty to drink.
In rustic cupfuls scooped from gurgling sedge,
ANDRÉS No ancient balladeer could say it better!
Next you can extol the emerald wonder
Of a fine and fragrant country meadow
That some fair lady's tread upon most finely
With her filthy, disgusting, shrunken toes.
CAPTAIN Let's stretch out on this grass, Don García,
Until someone comes along to guide us.
DON GARCÍA Sounds good to me.
ANDRÉS And even better to me.

(They stretch out on the grass.)

ANDRÉS The bellyful of wine I just gulped down
Will have to be my only blanket,

Gracias a Dios que me sacó tan presto
del engaño crüel de ser soldado
sujeto, sin ser fraile ni pupilo,
a tantas necedades y miserias.
Toda mi dicha estuvo en reformaros,
que luego al nuevo capitán y alférez
di trascartón, y quise ser más mozo
del camino que ser en la melicia
maese de campo de cuarenta tercios,
aunque pienso volverme a mis guitarras
y estar, pienso, en un carro más honrado,
que el sol es carretero y no soldado.

CAPITÁN ¿Qué hará Gileta agora, don García?

DON GARCÍA Lo que han hecho otras muchas, remendarse
y darse a un boquimuelle de su pueblo,
por sana de los pies y de las manos,
que eso duendes y lenguas hay muy pocos
que las entiendan ni las hayan visto.

ANDRÉS ¡Jo, Rucia! ¡Jo! ¡Te voto a Jerolisto!
¡Ah, mohína! ¡Par Dios, si me levanto!
¿Coces das?

DON GARCÍA Las aciones de los frenos
han rompido.

ANDRÉS ¡Jo, Rucia! ¡Jo, Mohína!

(Levántase ANDRÉS.)

CAPITÁN ¡Sueltas van!

ANDRÉS ¡El dïablo que las tenga
si de la sierra la vereda cogen!

Éntrase tras ellas ANDRÉS.

CAPITÁN Vámoslas a atajar por esta parte.

DON GARCÍA Dificultosas son. No pongas duda
de coger y mudar de pareceres
cuando se sueltan mulas y mujeres.

And this Lady Wineskin, my sweet pillow.
[Thank God I got out of being a soldier,
Subject to every endless misery,
Almost as bad as being a monk or student![107]
Yes, I played my hand pretty wisely
With Captain Carvajal and the Lieutenant,
Got bumped over to be their travelling boy
Rather than serving as an aide-de-camp,
At beck and call of forty different squadrons.
Still, I long to get back to my guitar.
Driving a cart's more honorable by far:
The sun shines on the carter, not the soldier,
And if you doubt it, go ask Apollo:
It was he who drove the world's first cart.][108]

CAPTAIN What do you think our little 'Gileta'
Is up to right now, Don García?

DON GARZÍA The same as so many women before her:
Making the best of her situation,
Giving herself over to some harmless peasant,
Some naïve idiot from her village.
And as for rumors, I don't believe them,
Or in magic, or evil spirits
Until I see it all with my own two eyes.

ANDRÉS Whoa, mules! Stupid beasts! Goddam you!
I'll take care of you! Stop your kicking!

DON GARCÍA They've broken their reins.

ANDRÉS Whoa, mules!

Andrés gets up.

CAPTAIN They're loose!

ANDRÉS If they stumble off the mountain path,
They'll be on the high road straight to hell!

Andrés exits after them.

CAPTAIN We can cut them off somewhere nearby.

DON GARCÍA They're rebellious. Change moods in a minute.
But what do you expect? They're just like women.

They exit.

Éntrense, y salgan agora LABRADORES cantando y bailando, y MADALENA y PASCUALA, niña, y lo que cantan es esto:

Salteóme la Serrana
juntico al pie de la cabaña.
Serrana, cuerpo garrido,
manos blancas, ojos bellidos,
salteóme en escondido
juntico al pie de la cabaña.
Salteóme la Serrana
juntico al pie de la cabaña.
Serrana, cuerpo lozana,
ojos negros, blancas manos,
salteóme en escampado
juntico al pie de la cabaña.
Salteóme la Serrana
juntico al pie de la cabaña.

MADALENA ¡Huyamos, porque esta fiera
sobre nosotros está,
y nadie se escapará
si fuese su padre!

Entre por abajo GILA. Huyen TODOS, y coge GILA a PASCUALA la niña.

GILA ¡Espera!
PASCUALA ¡Ay, desdichada de mí!
GILA ¿Qué temes? ¿No os santisface
que solo mi furor hace
mal a los hombres aquí,
y que a las mujeres no?
Que el que he de santisfacer
es agravio de mujer,
y soy la ofendida yo.
PASCUALA Hante pintado tan fiera,
Gila, que no hay de tu nombre
solmente quien no se asombre.
GILA Más blanda soy.
PASCUALA ¡Tirte huera
para quien huere tan boba
que se fíe de tu amor!

[Act Three, Scene 3. In the sierra.]

Enter villagers, singing and dancing, including Madalena and Pascuala, the little girl.[109] *They sing this:*

[VILLAGERS] I was assaulted by the Serrana
Just below her rustic cabin.
Serrana of beautiful eyes,
White hands and lovely body.
She assaulted me in secret
Just below her rustic cabin.
I was assaulted by the Serrana
Just below her rustic cabin.
Serrana of dark black eyes,
White hands, and shapely body.
She assaulted me in the clearing
Just below her rustic cabin.
I was assaulted by the Serrana
Just below her rustic cabin.[110]

MADALENA Here comes the she-beast! Run away![111]
No one escapes her, not even
Her own father!

Gila enters below. They all flee. Gila grabs Pascuala, the little girl.

GILA Wait!

PASCUALA Help me!

GILA Why do you tremble? Don't you know
My rage compels me to harm
Only men, never women?
The injury that was done to me
Is the injury done all women:
I suffer on behalf of us all.

PASCUALA They've made you out such a beast
That your name alone sparks terror
In every human being.

GILA I am far softer than that.

PASCUALA Get away! I'm not that stupid!
You can't be trusted. You have no love.

GILA Soldemente mi furor
a los hombres mata y roba,
que a las mujeres regalo.
Y con este ejemplo aviso.
PASCUALA La que engañan se lo quiso,
porque no hay hombre tan malo
que, cuando da la mujer
coces, la pueda ensillar.
GILA ¿Qué dicen en el lugar
de mí?
PASCUALA Que eres Locifer,
saltabardales, machorra,
el coco de las consejas,
el lobo de sus ovejas,
de las gallinas, la zorra.
Los niños callan contigo,
los hombres huyen de ti,
los viejos dicen que así
hue la Cava de Rodrigo,
las mozas, que otra pareja
no tuvo el mundo, y el cura
como ñublo te conjura
a la puerta de la igreja.
Cada vez que nuevas dan
de tu condición ingrata,
descomulgándote, mata
candelas el sacristán.
Y dicen que en haz y en paz
de toda esta serranía
te han de colgar algún día
como racimo de agraz.
GILA Como eso dirán de mí,
¿por qué a prenderme no vienen?
PASCUALA Gila, en veluntad lo tienen.
GILA ¡Vengan, pues, y desde allí
peñascos han de llover
por esta mano arrojados
que no dejen hombre!

GILA My rage drives me to rob and
Murder men and men alone.
I am generous to women,
Let this be my example.

PASCUALA Any woman who's been deceived
Has brought the deed upon herself.
There's no man strong or vile enough
To strap a saddle on a woman
When she's bucking and kicking.

GILA What do they say about me in town?

PASCUALA That you're Lucifer, a whore,
You're barren, you're the boogie man
Who haunts our dreams, the fox
Among hens, the wolf among sheep.
Children freeze when they hear your name.
Grown men go running and screaming.
Old folks think you're Caba, that witch
Who brought ruin to the Visigoths.
Young girls simply swear there's never
Been any woman like you – ever.
The priest stands at the church door, intoning
Endless litanies against you.
Every time new word gets out of
Your unfortunate situation,
The sexton snuffs out a candle,
Granting excommunication.
Yes, everywhere in this sierra,
People say you'll soon be hanging
Like a bunch of dried-up grapes.

GILA If that's what they say about me,
Why don't they arrest me?

PASCUALA Gila, that's what they want to do.

GILA Then let them give it a try!
I'll rain down boulders on their heads
Until not a single man is left.

PASCUALA Armados
cien hombres, escuché ayer,
que con la Santa Hermandad
de Plasencia andan tras ti.
Guárdate, Gila.
GILA ¡No vi
mayor donaire y beldad!
Decid, ¿de adónde, Pascuala,
toda esta gente venía?
PASCUALA Gila, de una romería,
que no ha quedado zagala
ni labrador en la villa
que no haya acudido allá.
GILA De esa fiesta tengo ya
noticia.
PASCUALA Y hue maravilla
dar con nosotros aquí,
siendo este tan apartado
camino.
GILA Tras un cuidado
que me trae fuera de mí,
que debió ser fantasía
de mi loco pensamiento,
bajé aquí imitando el viento.
Ya se va acabando el día.
Vete, Pascuala.
PASCUALA Adiós, pues.
GILA ¿Sabrás el camino?
PASCUALA Sí,
y hay muy poco desde aquí
al lugar.
GILA Si acaso ves
a mi padre, no le digas
que me has visto ni encontrado.
PASCUALA Él está contigo airado.
¿Picándote están ortigas?
GILA No. Estoy muy segura aquí,
puesto que si me acomete

PASCUALA Just yesterday, I heard a hundred
Heavily armed men from the Holy
Brotherhood of Plasencia
Were on your trail. Beware of them!
GILA I've never seen such beauty and grace.
Where are these people coming from?
PASCUALA From a romería, Gila.
Every girl and boy in town has
Joined in the joyous pilgrimage.
GILA I heard word of this fiesta.
PASCUALA It was truly a miracle
You came across us today.
This path is so distant and remote.
GILA Deciding to imitate the wind,
I descended in pursuit
Of a strange obsession that
Turned out to be a fantasy,
A reverie inspired by
My crazed imagination.
Daylight dwindles. Go, Pascuala.
PASCUALA Goodbye, then.
GILA You know the road?
PASCUALA Yes, it's not a long way home.
GILA Don't tell my father you saw me.
PASCUALA He's out of his mind with rage at you.
Do those thorny soldiers prick you?
GILA No. I'm very safe up here.
The whole world can attack me,

el mundo, no importa. Vete,
y a los del lugar les di
que se guarden de mí.

PASCUALA Adiós.

Vase yendo la niña PASCUALA.

GILA ¡Y que si dan en hablar,
que iré a abrasar el lugar!

PASCUALA ¡Malos años para vos!

GILA ¿Mi furor no te acobarda?

PASCUALA Alcanzarme es por demás,
Gila. Aquí reganarás
con sal y vinagre.

GILA ¡Aguarda!

Vase la NIÑA corriendo.

¡Notable gracia ha tenido!
La noche baja. Yo quiero
retirarme.

Entre ANDRÉS solo agora.

ANDRÉS Desespero.
Cansado vengo, y rendido.
Las mulas se han despeñado
de esta sierra áspera y fría,
o para desdicha mía
la tierra las ha tragado.
Al dïablo doy oficio
de tanta costa de pies,
y de tan poco interés
vengo perdiendo el jüicio.
¡Vive Dios, si contra mí
un millón de hombres bajara,
que con todos me matara!
Una mujer está aquí.

GILA Este ha perdido el camino
y ha dado con gentil guía.

ANDRÉS ¿A quién digo? ¡Ah, tía! ¡Ah, tía!

It makes no difference at all.
Go, tell everyone in town
To beware of me.

PASCUALA Goodbye.

Pascuala, the little girl, starts going.

GILA And if they keep saying those things
About me, I'll burn the whole town
To the ground!

PASCUALA Curse you, if you do!

[GILA My rage doesn't make you cower?

PASCUALA No use trying to catch me, Gila.
Find another pair of eyes
To rub your piss and vinegar!

GILA Wait!

The girl exits running.

GILA She had a certain grace to her.
Night falls. Time to retire.

Enter Andrés, alone now.

ANDRÉS I'm desperate, worn out, exhausted.
The mules jumped off a cliff somewhere,
The cold earth gobbled them up.
To hell with this profession of
Aching feet and empty pockets!
I'm on the verge of losing my mind.
If a million men stood in my way,][112]
I'd die fighting every last one!
Wait. I see a woman.

GILA [aside] This man seems to have lost his way.
He's come across the perfect guide.

ANDRÉS Who's that? Mommy? Yoo-hoo?

GILA ¿Qué es lo que mandáis, sobrino?
ANDRÉS ¿Habéis visto por aquí
dos mulas?
GILA Cada momento
encuentro bestias.
ANDRÉS ¡Contento
para pullas vengo!
GILA A mí
me pesa que no vengáis
de muy buen gusto. ¿Sois mozo
de mulas?
ANDRÉS ¡Lindo escorrozo!
¡Soy el dïablo!
GILA No habláis,
para hombre de bien, muy bien.
ANDRÉS ¡Oh, cuerpo de Dios con ella!
¿Qué he de hablar cuando la estrella
de Venus en la sartén
de la noche con las otras
sale a estrellarse, y yo estoy
de la manera que voy,
las plantas llenas de potras,
como ell ánima, también
cansado, errado el camino,
sin mulas y con poco vino?
Mirad con quién y sin quién.
GILA Ya es fuerza tener paciencia,
pues que no podéis llegar
agora a ningún lugar,
a La Venta ni a Plasencia,
yo os daré donde esta noche
paséis muy bien y cenéis,
y con el alba saldréis.
ANDRÉS Cuando tendido en un coche
o en una litera fuera,
el hospedaje acetara.
¿Dormís sola, linda cara?
GILA No hay serrana de la Vera

GILA How can I help you, daddy?
ANDRÉS Have you seen a pair of mules?
GILA All I see is an ugly beast.
ANDRÉS I'm in no mood for jokes.
GILA So you're not happy to see me?
Aren't you a little mule boy?
ANDRÉS Very funny. I'm the devil.
GILA For a man of such good renown,
You don't talk very good.
ANDRÉS May the body of Christ be on her!
How am I supposed to talk
With Venus sloshing around
In her watery dipper and
Every last star curdling
In the milky way above?
I'm stuck out here, like you see,
The soles of my feet ripped to shreds,
And my spirits shredded too;
I'm exhausted, on the wrong road,
No mules, almost out of wine,
Just me, myself, and I – and you!
GILA You'll need to try a little patience.
You're not getting to La Venta
Or Plasencia tonight.
But I can offer you a place
To spend a pleasant evening
And eat a tasty dinner
And stay until break of dawn.
ANDRÉS When you're stranded on the road,
Without coach, without carriage,
You accept whatever marriage
Of convenience you are offered.
Are you sleeping alone, sweet thing?
GILA There's no serrana in la Vera

que acudir más libre pueda
a lo que fuerdes servido,
porque me habéis parecido
muy bien.

ANDRÉS ¡Hoy pongo a la rueda
de la Fortuna mil clavos!
¡Perdello todo es razón,
pues de vuestros ojos son
mis pensamientos esclavos!

GILA Comenzá a subir.

ANDRÉS ¿Por dónde?

GILA Por esas peñas, que allí
tengo yo mi choza.

ANDRÉS Así,
pues tu amor me corresponde,
estuviera sobre el sol,
y aun sobre el sol fa mi ré,
que allá entrara, por la fe
de soldado y español.

GILA Sube.

ANDRÉS Ya voy agarrando.

GILA Pues te cansas, dueño mío,
desde este peñasco al río
quiero que bajes volando.

ANDRÉS ¡No me despeñes, espera!
¿Quién eres, mujer ingrata?

GILA ¡Gila, fanfarrón! ¡Te mata
la Serrana de la Vera!

(Arrójale, y dice luego:)

Esto bastará por hoy,
porque ya la sombra obscura
vestir los montes procura
de miedo y luto, y yo soy
de poco provecho aquí
si nuevos lances espero.
Entrarme en mi choza quiero
y esperar al sol allí

Who would more freely serve
Your each and every need.
You look just fine to me.

ANDRÉS I'm ready to roll the dice
And wager everything I've got!
My imagination is enslaved
By dreams of your deep, dark eyes.

GILA Come on up.

ANDRÉS Where?

GILA Up this ridge
My cabin's at the top of the cliff.

ANDRÉS Since we seem to be in harmony,
I'll climb singing do, re, mi,
I swear as a soldier and Spaniard!

GILA Come up!

ANDRÉS I'm down on all fours.

GILA Instead of crawling, tired sweetheart,
Why don't you take wing and fly
Off this cliff and down to the river?

ANDRÉS Wait! Please! Don't push me off!
Who are you, ungrateful woman?

GILA Gila, you boasting bully.
You are about to killed by
La Serrana de la Vera,

(She throws him off, then says:)

GILA That's enough work for today.
Shadows drape the darkening hills,
Cloaking them in terror and grief.
[No more profit left for me.
Time to go into my cabin
And await another sunrise,

para volver a buscar
vidas, Gila, en que te cebes.
¡Ah, noche!, lo que me debes,
¿cuándo me lo has de pagar?

Éntrese en su choza, y salga DON LUCAS, perdido, diciendo:

CAPITÁN ¡Noche obscura! ¡Ah, madre helada
del engaño y la ocasión
que al amante y al ladrón
das de una suerte posada
de cuya capa estrellada
se visten tantas traiciones,
tantas varias invenciones,
tantos ardides y enredos,
tantas vergüenzas y miedos,
tanto honor en opiniones!,
¿dónde me vas remontando
del camino y del lugar,
que por preciarte de errar
quieres que camine errando,
que voy perdiendo y buscando,
entre peñascos y estrellas,
de ellos espantadas ellas,
de ellas ellos respetados
tanto, que están coronados
de sus blancas luces bellas?
En ese jaral espeso
perdí al tramontar de día
con el sol a don García,
que iguala un propio suceso.
Que voy con miedo confieso.
No hay rama que se me ofrezca
que un hombre no me parezca.
¡Oh, si el alba con llorar
perlas diese en sobornar
al sol para que amanezca!

When I can venture out in search of lives
To satiate my hunger.
O night, how you are in my debt!
When will you ever you pay me back?][113]

She enters her cabin. Enter Don Lucas, lost, saying:

CAPTAIN Cold, dark night! Mother of deceit![114]
You shelter both lover and thief,
Giving opportunity to each.
Your starry cape cloaks a hundred
Thousand lies and treacheries.
O the many machinations,
O the varied ruses and schemes,
The countless acts of shame and fear,
And the honor that's been squandered!
To where do you carry me off,
Leaving road and town behind?
To what remote forest are we bound?
Erring is this errant traveler,
Wandering in your dark wonder;
The more I try to find my way,
The more I lose myself amid
Lofty stars and precipice.
Those stars are surely terrified
By the sight of each precipice,
Yet those cliffs must pay respect
To that radiant light from above.
As the sun fled from the sky,
I found myself deeply folded
Into this rock rose thicket.
I lost Don García too –
Surely he's lost the same as I.
I confess, I'm terrified.
Every branch before my face
Becomes the menacing embrace
Of men who mean to do me harm.
O daybreak, with your pearls of dew,
Would you the bribe the sun into dawning?

Todo con la sombra vana
me altera y me desconfía.
Hidalga cosa es el día
cuanto es la noche villana.
¡Oh, sol, de la espuma cana
saca tu roja cabeza!
¡Restituye la belleza
que robó la sombra escura
porque venza tu hermosura
a su cobarde tristeza!
¡Mal haya, amén, la ocasión
de desatinos iguales!,
pero quien sigue animales
merece este galardón.
Altas estas peñas son.
No hay camino por aquí.
Parece que siento allí
luz. Aunque lejos está,
he de caminar allá.
¿Lumbre es de pastores? Sí.
Cabaña debe de ser.
Parece que está en el cielo.
Que pueda llegar recelo,
aunque he de hacer por poder,
que mejor podré tener
la noche allí que en la sierra,
donde me aperciben guerra
miedo, sueño y noche fría,
que presto el sol con el día
del mar saltará a la tierra.

(Llegue tentando.)

¡Gracias a Dios que llegué!
Esta es la puerta. Durmiendo
deben de estar. Yo pretendo
llamar, que esta dicha fue.
De la noche pasaré
aquí lo que queda ya.

[In these shadows, everything morphs,
Nothing is firm, nothing trusted.
Day is an honest gentleman
Compared to this rogue called the night.
Lift your golden locks, o sun!
Restore to earth the loveliness!
Let your beauty wash triumphant
Over this cowering darkness!][115]
Damn this cursed situation!
But he who trusts in animals
Deserves to reap this rich reward.
These cliffs all around me are high,
There's no road anywhere in sight.
Wait – I think I spy the light
Of some humble shepherd's campfire.
Seems far away. I'll walk there.
It seems to be some kind of cabin.
It looks like a slice of heaven.
Should be cautious – but what are my options?
Better than spending a night out here,
Subject to cold, to nightmares, and
The loaded guns of drunken soldiers.
I can rest there until the sun
Clambers up over the eastern sea
And leaps back onto the land.

(The Captain arrives, feeling his way.)

This is the door. I've made it!
They must be asleep. I'll knock.
Finally, I stumbled on some luck
Where I can spend what's left of the night.

(Llama el CAPITÁN, y responde GILA de adentro:)

¡Ah, de la choza!
GILA ¿Quién va?
CAPITÁN Amigos.
GILA No puede ser,
mas yo me levanto a ver
quién ese nombre se da.
CAPITÁN La voz que me ha respondido
dentro de aquesta cabaña,
si el sentido no me engaña,
de mujer me ha parecido.
Mas si el haberme perdido
fuese de importancia alguna
para darme la Fortuna
alguna hermosa serrana
con quien la alegre mañana
me pareciese importuna,
que toda esta Vera da,
entre los muchos frutales,
hermosuras celestiales,
y alguna en la sierra está.
La puerta han abierto ya.

Salga GILA, con la escopeta, a la puerta.

GILA ¿Quién es?
CAPITÁN Un perdido soy,
que no acierto dónde estoy.
GILA ¿Dónde vais que así os perdéis?
CAPITÁN Mujer es.
GILA ¿No respondéis?
CAPITÁN Serrana, a Plasencia voy.
GILA Pues ¿qué os trujo por aquí?
CAPITÁN Perdí las mulas ayer,
y un amigo por correr
tras ellas, y me perdí
justamente, pues así
perdido supe ganarme,
pues a perderme y hallarme
vengo en vos, serrana mía.

(The Captain knocks. Gila responds from offstage.)

CAPTAIN Anyone home?
GILA *[off]* Who's there?
CAPTAIN A friend!
GILA *[off]* I doubt it. But I'll go get it
And see who dares claim that name.
CAPTAIN It seems to be a woman's voice.
I've found good fortune after all –
To get lost, and come across
A beautiful serrana!
Morning might come with regrets
If I'm not up for parting yet.
This fertile Vera's famed for yielding
Juicy and delicious fruit,
Plucked at the highest elevation.
The door is opening.

Enter Gila with the rifle, in the doorway.

GILA Who is it?
CAPTAIN A lost man. I don't know where I am.
GILA Where were you headed, when you got lost?
CAPTAIN *[aside]* It is a woman.
GILA Why won't you answer?
CAPTAIN I'm bound for Plasencia.
GILA What brings you up this way?
CAPTAIN I lost my mules early in the day,
Along with a good friend of mine
Who went chasing after them.
But though I'm lost, I have won,
For in losing myself, I now find
Myself by your side.

GILA Esa voz conozco.
CAPITÁN El día
con vos podrá acreditarme,
porque soy hombre de bien
y el talle es información.
GILA Muy pocos hombres lo son,
aunque lo dicen también.
CAPITÁN El comenzar por desdén
es señal que he de ganar.
GILA Tahur os queréis mostrar
de amor.
CAPITÁN Soy acuchillado.
GILA ¿Sois de Plasencia?
CAPITÁN Y honrado.
¿Conocéis en el lugar
gente?
GILA A los más principales
que Plasencia sangre dio,
con tanto valor.
CAPITÁN Pues yo
soy de los Carvajales.
GILA Al mismo Rey son iguales.
¿Qué nombre tenéis?
CAPITÁN Serrana,
don Lucas.
GILA No salió vana
mi sospecha.
CAPITÁN De la guerra
vuelvo a vivir a mi tierra
y a retirarme con gana
de tomar en ella estado,
de una hermosa compañía
que saqué de infantería
de la Vera, reformado.
GILA A buen puerto habéis llegado.
(Ap.: Noche, piedad has tenido,
pues que me has restituido
la ocasión que me debías

GILA *(aside)* I know that voice.
CAPTAIN Extend me some credit for the night.
I call on daylight to vouch for me –
When it shines its morning light,
Revealing me in fullest figure,
This message will be delivered:
I am a respectable man.
GILA Many are the men who claim to be,
Few are the men who are.
CAPTAIN *(aside)* Feigning disdain,
The old rouse: a certain sign
I'm going to have my way.
GILA You're ready to gamble on love?
CAPTAIN How can I not? I'm stabbed in the heart.
GILA Are you from Plasencia?
CAPTAIN Yes, and greatly honored there.
Do you know anyone from there?
GILA I know all its leading people
Who valiantly gave their blood.
CAPTAIN Well, I am a Carvajal.
GILA They are equals to the King.
What's your name?
CAPTAIN I am Don Lucas.
GILA *[aside]* My suspicions were not in vain.
CAPTAIN I'm on my way back from the war,
Wanting to settle down in peace
In the homeland that I love,
Relinquishing the beautiful
Company of fighting men
That I mustered in La Vera.[116]
GILA You've docked at the right port.
(aside) Night, you've been most merciful,
Restoring my chance for revenge,
Revenge that I long longed for.

para las venganzas mías,
aunque en largas me has traído.
Hoy contigo cuentas hago,
y pues satisfecha estoy
de lo que me debes, hoy
te daré carta de pago,
que aunque es mejor el estrago
de las costas que te he hecho
por cobrar de ti, sospecho,
según duró mi esperanza,
que no llega la venganza
al agravio de mi pecho.)

CAPITÁN Serrana, suspensa estás.
Si satisfecha de mí
me quisieres dar aquí
posada, merced me harás.

GILA Ya no han de engañarme más,
porque de uno me fïé
como vos, y de él quedé,
de que me quiso engañada,
infamemente burlada,
y él a la guerra se hue,
que era también capitán
como vos, y se llamaba
don Lucas, y se preciaba
del apellido que os dan,
muy traidor y muy galán,
muy noble y muy fementido,
muy falso y muy bien nacido,
muy valiente y muy crüel,
y a la he, si no sois él,
que me lo habéis parecido.

CAPITÁN *(Ap.:* ¡En notable confusión
este suceso me ha puesto!
¡Sueño parece que es esto,
pintura, imaginación!

Who knows why you led me astray
Only to put this before me now?
[Tonight I settle accounts with you.
I am satisfied you will pay in full,
And so I submit my bill:
Be assured your depredations
Have cost me more than you can pay.
I've waited so long for this moment,
Mere revenge can never settle
The grievance seething in my breast.][117]

CAPTAIN Serrana, you seem distracted.
Do you need proof of who I am?
Offer me your shelter here,
Shower me with your sweet mercy,
And you will see the man I am.

GILA I will no longer be deceived,
I once trusted someone like you,
And I ended up deceived,
Cruelly mocked, humiliated,
Exactly as the man intended.
Then the man went off to war –
He was a captain just like you,
And he called himself Don Lucas,
And he also used his family name
To boast and brag and lord it.
He was a very gallant man
And very much a traitor;
He was a fine nobleman,
And very much a liar –
Born to the best of families,
Yet prone to the worst of falsehoods.
He was valiant – and he was cruel.
And I swear to God, looking at you,
I see exactly that man.

CAPTAIN *(aside)* I'm astounded and confused
By this stunning circumstance:
It's like a dream, a fiction,
A work of pure imagination,

¡Gila es esta, y estas son
quejas de que dueño he sido!
¡A gentil puerto he venido!
Pero, ¿qué puerto ha de hallar
quien de la noche en el mar
corre tormenta perdido?
Y apelar a bien no espero,
pues de plano he confesado.)

GILA Vos parecéis hombre honrado
y daros posada quiero.

CAPITÁN No, serrana, que el lucero
de la aurora desafía
a la noche con el día.
Yo agradezco ese favor.
Quedaos a Dios.

GILA No, señor.
Mi güesped habéis de ser.

CAPITÁN Estáis sola y sois mujer,
y yo estimo vuestro honor.

GILA ¿De cuándo acá lo estimáis?

CAPITÁN Desde el día en que nací.

GILA ¡Mentís, que hay testigo aquí
de que verdades no habláis!
Yo soy Gila, a quien estáis
deudor de tan justa queja,
que el delito os aconseja
lo mismo que vos hüís,
y a la cárcel os venís
por entraros en la igreja.
Que el Cielo, a quien traidor huistes,
con esta noche me ampara,
porque en ella me vengara
de la que vos me ofendistes.
Y puesto que os encubristes
con la mentirosa capa
que tantos delitos tapa,
de tal manera saltea,
roba mi honor y capea,

This is Gila! And I must own
All of her accusations.
Adrift in the stormy sea of night,
Look at the port at which I've docked!
I have no means of appeal,
I've already made my confession.

GILA You seem an honorable man.
I'm happy to give you shelter.

CAPTAIN No, serrana, the morning star
Is now disputing with the night
Over the right to break the dawn.
I appreciate this favor.
God be with you.

GILA No, señor,
I insist: please be my guest.

CAPTAIN You're a woman, you're all alone.
I'm a man, must respect your honor.

GILA When did you suddenly decide
To be so respectful?

CAPTAIN I've been a
Respectful man since the day I was born.

GILA You lie. There's a witness here
To truths you dare not speak aloud.
I am Gila, and you are in debt
To me beyond all doubt.
Your crime counsels you to flee,
But this cell, which you now enter,
Beckons you to confession.
[Heaven now is on my side:
As a traitor, you fled from its light.
Now it protects me with its night,
And in this night I take revenge.
You cloaked yourself in its cape of lies,
Assaulting my honor to your content
And then bidding a hasty retreat
In the fading fabric of its cape.

que aun la noche no se escapa,
hoy de los hombros le quito
la capa a la noche fría,
aunque lo mismo hace el día
que en esta ocasión imito.
Mi venganza solicito,
y en estando yo vengada,
los ejes de la estrellada
fábrica sobre mí den,
porque no espera otro bien
una mujer agraviada.

CAPITÁN Gila, palabra te di
de ser tu esposo. Aquí estoy,
tu esposo y tu esclavo soy.

GILA Ya es tarde, ingrato. De aquí
has de volar, pues por ti
al Cielo he sido traidora
con tantas culpas.

CAPITÁN ¡Señora!

GILA ¡No hay ruegos que mi honor estrague!
¡Quien tal hace, que tal pague,
y cáigase el Cielo agora!

Arrójale y luego dicen de adentro, por arriba y por abajo, cogiéndola en medio:

CUADRILLERO 1.º ¡Esta es su choza!

DON JUAN ¡Abrasalda!

GILA Ya no hay temor que altere.

DON JUAN ¡Cuando darse no quisiere,
muera! ¡Abrasalda, quemalda!

GILA Por la cumbre y por la falda
vienen a cogerme en medio.
Ya no hay de escapar remedio.

Por arriba CUADRILLEROS, con arcabuces, y por abajo también, y con ellos, DON JUAN DE CARVAJAL, alcalde de la Hermandad de Plasencia, y GIRALDO, padre de GILA, también con su vara, y MINGO también, como cuadrillero.

Night is no longer your escape.][118]
In this cold night I take this cape
Off your shoulders, just as darkness
Is uncloaked by the truth of day.
I seek my revenge, and once avenged,
May the axes of this starry sky
The fabric of the firmament,
Fall upon me from on high:
A woman who's been affronted
Can seek no other fortune.

CAPTAIN Gila, I gave you my word
To be your loyal husband.
I stand here before you now:
Your husband and your slave.

GILA Too late, ungrateful man.
It's time for you to fly away,
From this same spot where I've betrayed
God with so many sins.

CAPTAIN Señora!

GILA My honor makes a ruin
Of your each and every plea!
We pay a price for what we've done.
Let Heaven come crashing down on us!

She throws him off the cliff. Then off stage, from above and below, come voices, trapping her in the middle:

1ST TROOPER *[off]* This is her cabin!

DON JUAN *[off]* Burn it down!

GILA I am beyond all fear.

DON JUAN *[off]* If she refuses to surrender,
Kill her. Burn the place down!

GILA They come from below and above,
Mountain foot and mountain peak.
I am trapped. There is no escape.

From above and below, enter troops with arquebuses. With them is Don Juan de Carvajal, leader of the Brotherhood of Plasencia, and Giraldo, Gila's father, with his staff of office, and Mingo, also a troop member.

MINGO ¡Aquí está!
DON JUAN ¡Llegad, llegad!
¡Tente a la Santa Hermandad!
GILA ¿Qué haré?, que romper por medio
es imposible. Ya estoy
vengada, y esto ha de ser.
GIRALDO ¡Acaba! ¡Date, mujer!
GILA Tu hija pienso que soy.
GIRALDO Ese nombre no te doy
por las crueldades que has hecho.
Tú eres hija de ese pecho
crüel, que no pude yo
engendrarte.
GILA ¿Por qué no,
si me ha forzado mi afrenta?
GIRALDO Al cielo darás la cuenta,
pues tu castigo llegó,
que ha permitido que venga
a prenderte yo también.
GILA Padre, habéis hecho muy bien.
GIRALDO Tu engaño no nos detenga.
Date a prisión.
GILA Hoy se venga
mi honor, y llega con él
de la Fortuna crüel,
la temida ejecución.
DON JUAN ¡Acaba! ¡Date a prisión!
GILA Las manos rindo al cordel.
DON JUAN Rinde las armas primero.
GILA ¿Aun teméis con tanta gente?
A mi padre solamente
rendir las armas espero,
que aunque vos sois caballero,
para mí es mi padre más.
GIRALDO ¡Muestra!

MINGO Here's her place.
DON JUAN Approach, men.
Surrender to the Brotherhood!
GILA What do I do? Every way is blocked.
I have gotten my revenge.
What must be, must be.
GIRALDO Stop right there!
Give yourself up right now, woman!
GILA Daughter, I believe, is the word.
GIRALDO For your many inhuman acts,
I refuse you that name, I refuse.
You are daughter only to
Your own despicable breast.
I could not have engendered you.
GILA Didn't you force this affront upon me?
GIRALDO Your day of punishment has arrived.
Settle your account with God.
I thank God too, I've been allowed
To take part in capturing you.
GILA Well done, father.
GIRALDO Let's not be delayed
By her lies and deceptions.
Surrender. You're going to prison.
GILA My honor has been avenged,
Brought to fearful fruition by
The unrelenting wheel of fortune.
DON JUAN Enough of this! Take her to prison!
GILA I offer up both my hands to
These binding cords of justice.
DON JUAN Surrender your arms first.
GILA Accompanied by so many men,
And still you're afraid of me?
I intend to surrender my arms –
But only to this man, my father,
You may be a gentleman,
But my father is a nobleman
To me.
GIRALDO Hold your hands up high!

DON JUAN ¡No he visto jamás
en hombre tanto valor!

(Dale a GIRALDO la escopeta y el cuchillo de monte.)

GILA Vengué, en efeto, mi honor.
DON JUAN ¡Esposas!
MINGO Perdonarás
a Mingo este atrevimiento,
porque me han cabido a mí.
GILA Si yo te matara a ti,
escusara el cumplimiento.

(Pónele las esposas.)

DON JUAN ¡Grillos y cadenas!
GILA El viento
no me llevará, señor
Alcalde.
DON JUAN ¡Estraño valor!
GILA No hay sino tener paciencia.

(Pónenle a los pies los grillos y una cadena.)

CUADRILLERO. Ya está esto puesto.
DON JUAN ¡A Plasencia!
GILA Vengué, en efeto, mi honor.

Vanse TODOS, rodeando a GILA con los arcabuces, y salga DON FERNANDO, y DOÑA ISABEL.

FERNANDO ¡No se puede pintar la gallardía,
la belleza y valor de la Serrana!
ISABEL ¡Celos me dais, por vuestra vida y mía!
FERNANDO ¿A vos os puede dar mujer humana
celos, siendo vos cielo de mis ojos?
ISABEL Tal vez suele agradar una villana
como tosco manjar, que por antojos
da el harto del faisán al apetito.
FERNANDO Nunca al amor da el gusto esos enojos,
mas necio vengo a ser, pues solicito

DON JUAN No man could show greater courage.

(She gives Giraldo the rifle and the mountain knife.)

GILA I avenged my own honor.
DON JUAN Handcuffs!
MINGO You'll pardon Mingo this presumption
Of being present – he was in
The wrong place at the wrong time.
GILA I should have killed you, and saved you
That presumption.

(He puts the handcuffs on her.)

DON JUAN Shackles and chains!
GILA I'm not going to fly away
In the wind, señor.
DON JUAN What courage!
GILA It's just that I have endless patience.

(They put shackles and a chain on her feet.)

TROOPER They're on.
DON JUAN To Plasencia!
GILA I avenged my own honor.

Surrounding Gila with the arquebuses, they all exit.

[Act Three, Scene 4. Ferdinand and Isabella's court.][119]

Enter Ferdinand and Isabella.

FERDINAND It's absolutely beyond any description:[120]
That Serrana's elegance and courage.
ISABELLA On my life, you are making me jealous.
FERDINAND A mere woman, here on earth, makes you jealous
When you are heaven itself in my eyes?
ISABELLA Sometimes even a peasant can be pleasing,
Like some simple, rustic morsel that serves
As appetizer to the roasted pheasant.
FERDINAND Such morsels irritate the stomach:
They add no flavor to the banquet of love.

daros satisfación, Isabel mía,
del que vos conocéis, y es infinito.
Dadme esos brazos porque envidie el día
lo que yo os diere a vos, si la Serrana
a celos con mi amor os desafía,
que por la vida de Isabel y Juana,
que voy con intención de que se prenda,
porque demás de ser tan inhumana,
no hay en la Vera de Plasencia senda
ni camino que de ella está seguro.

ISABEL Pues la Hermandad es bien que en eso entienda.

FERNANDO Sírvenle de defensa y alto muro
esa sierra en que está, y así es en vano
el llegalla a prender, mas yo procuro
con cuatro compañías desde el llano
batirle esos peñascos.

Sale DON RODRIGO GIRÓN.

ISABEL ¿Qué hay, Maestre?

DON RODRIGO La Hermandad de Plasencia, que con mano
armada asalta esa muralla alpestre
de esos riscos, ha preso a la Serrana,
porque el valor de la Hermandad se muestre,
llevándola a Plasencia esta mañana,
adonde habrán de hacer justicia de ella
sino es que apela a la piedad cristiana
de vuestros pechos.

FERNANDO La común querella,
los atroces delitos no permiten
que se tenga piedad, Girón, con ella,
y no es razón que a la Hermandad le quiten,
pues que tan nueva está, las esenciones
que vuestros previlegios les admiten.
Castiguen como es justo a los ladrones,
sin que haya apelación, que de esta suerte
se evitarán muy grandes ocasiones
fuera de que esta ha dado a muchos muerte

But now I'm babbling like an idiot:
You know my love for you is infinite.
Let me prove it again. Give me your arms.
The sun itself shall envy the offering
That, brightly shining, I now bestow you.
If this Serrana provokes such jealousy
I hereby swear by the names of Isabella
And Juana that I have given the royal order
For her arrest. The woman is inhuman,
And there is no road in all La Vera
Safe from her cruelty and predations.

ISABELLA I hope the Brotherhood has been informed.

FERDINAND The rampart of the sierra is her defense.
No one has managed to apprehend her.
But I have assembled four fresh companies
Who will rise up from these lowly valleys
To give her battle on those ferocious heights.

Enter Don Rodrigo Girón.

ISABELLA What news do you bring, good Master?

DON RODRIGO The Brotherhood
Of Plasencia launched an armed assault
On the high sierra's loftiest wall.
The Serrana is now their prisoner,
And they are bringing her to Plasencia
In a show of valor, this very morning.
There, they will serve public justice on her,
Unless she appeals to the Christian compassion
That resides within your noble breasts.

FERDINAND The collective petition, not to mention
The horrifying crimes and accusations,
Allow for no such compassion, good Girón.
The Brotherhood must maintain its position:
It is, after all, a new institution, and
We must respect the privileges we granted.[121]
They have the right to punish thieves without appeal,
And this case involves far more than a thief –
Indeed, she's murdered many, many men.

y la merece por razón de estado.
DON RODRIGO Con intención justísima lo advierte
Vuestra Alteza, señor.
ISABEL Pena me ha dado,
sabiendo que es mujer.
NUÑO. Ya las literas
aguardan y las guardas han llegado.
FERNANDO Partamos a Plasencia. Las primeras
sospechas brevemente desengañan.
ISABEL No las tuve jamás por verdaderas,
aunque el amor los celos acompañan.

Éntrense.

Salga DON GARCÍA solo.

DON GARCÍA Perdido ya de dos días,
vengo a dar en las murallas
de Plasencia sin saber
de Andrés ni de don Lucas nada,
de las mulas, ni de mí,
que aun pienso que no se acaban
los jarales y las peñas
de estas dos noches pasadas.
Temo, por lo que han dicho
de Gila, de la serrana
a quien don Lucas burló,
no haya tomado venganza,
pues por esta causa solo
en la sierra salteaba,
y sin querer ni sabello
perdido pudo encontralla.
De la ciudad sale gente.
Quiero saber a qué causa,
que me parece en la prisa
novedad.

MADALENA y PASCUALA.

	It clearly merits punishment by the state.
DON RODRIGO	Your grasp of the circumstance is most just.
ISABELLA	This news grieves me. She is a woman.

[Enter Don Nuño.]

DON NUÑO	The litters are waiting. The guard has arrived.
FERDINAND	Let's go immediately to Plasencia. Your jealousy will vanish in an instant.
ISABELLA	You took my jealousy far too seriously. Love and jealousy keep close company.

[They exit.][122]

[Act Three, Scene 5. The outskirts of Plasencia.]

Enter Don García, alone.

DON GARCÍA I've been lost for two whole days,[123]
And finally I stumble on
Plasencia's sainted walls.
Who knows what happened to Andrés,
Or the mules, or Don Lucas.
I don't even know what happened
To me, I still see myself
Stumbling around in the darkness
Of endless rock rose thickets,
Teetering along the edges
Of enormous ledges and cliffs.
From everything I know of Gila,
I'm sure she's gotten her revenge
On Don Lucas, for his act of
Mockery and humiliation,
Which, after all, was the reason
She took to assaulting men.
He could have come upon her blindly.
Here come people, from the city.
I wonder why they're rushing about.

Enter Madalena and Pascuala.

MADALENA ¡Anda, Pascuala!
PASCUALA No voy, de pesar, en mí.
DON GARCÍA ¿Qué es esto, hermosas serranas?
MADALENA Es la desdicha mayor
que se ha visto.
DON GARCÍA ¿Cómo?
MADALENA Sacan
a josticiar aquí huera
de la ciudad, como manda
la Santa Hermandad, a Gila,
esa serrana gallarda
que entre Garganta la Olla
y Plasencia salteaba.
Don Juan de Carvajal,
que es Alcalde de la Santa
Hermandad, la prendió, y toda
la de la Vera es su guarda,
que, de haber muerto a don Lucas,
su primo, toma venganza
con esto.
DON GARCÍA ¿A don Lucas dices
que ha muerto?
MADALENA Esa es cosa crara.
Quedaos a Dios, que ya llega.
PASCUALA Vamos.

(Pónganse PASCUALA a un lado, y MADALENA en el tablado.)

DON GARCÍA Nunca miente el alma.
¡Parece sueño! Las nuevas,
aunque de mí receladas,
me han dejado sin sentido.
Vengóse al fin la Serrana.
Dios te perdone don Lucas,
de tantas desdichas causa.

Éntrese DON GARCÍA, y suenen agora campanillas, y salgan CUADRILLEROS, con ballestas y flechas en ellas, capotes verdes de dos faldas, luego GILA, con esposas en lasmanos, como la prendieron, Y DON JUAN, con vara, detrás, de negro, vestido con ferreruelo, y GIRALDO, con vara también.

MADALENA Come on, Pascuala!
PASCUALA I'm out of my mind.
DON GARCÍA What's this, my beautiful serranas?
MADALENA The most terrible thing that
I've ever seen.
DON GARCÍA And what's that?
MADALENA They're making her face justice,
Here, outside the city walls,
As the Holy Brotherhood decrees –
Gila, the gallant serrana,
Who assaulted men between Plasencia
And Garganta la Olla.
The leader of the Brotherhood
Is the man who captured her:
Don Juan de Carvajal.
He's joined by a company of
Men from all over La Vera.
She killed his cousin, Don Lucas,
And he will have his revenge.
DON GARCÍA You say she killed Don Lucas?
MADALENA That's for certain. Here they come.
Goodbye!
PASCUALA Let's go already!

(Pascuala moves to one side, while Madalena stays on stage.)

DON GARCÍA The soul never lies. I knew it.
Yet it seems like a strange dream.
Can I trust this piece of news?
It leaves me senseless, and yet –
She got her revenge in the end.
God forgive you, Don Lucas,
For causing all this misfortune.

Exit Don García. Drums sound. Enter troops with crossbows, and green two-sided hoods. Then Gila in handcuffs, the same as when they caught her. Behind her enters Don Juan with his staff of office, dressed in black ferreruelo, along with Giraldo, with his staff too.

GILA — Nadie de mí se lastime,
los que me ven tan amarga
muerte morir, porque yo
no la tengo por desgracia.
Contenta muero, por ver
que el Cielo, con esta traza
de mi predestinación,
el bien que mi muerte aguarda,
que de otra suerte parece
que fuera imposible, a causa
de los delitos que he hecho
solo por tomar venganza,
que sin robos y salteos,
por estas manos ingratas
tengo a cargo dos mil vidas
de que pido perdón.

PASCUALA — ¡Rasgan,
Madalena, el corazón
sus razones!

MADALENA — Sí, Pascuala.

GILA — ¡Ah, padre! ¡Ah, señor!

GIRALDO — ¿Qué quieres?

GILA — Escúchame una palabra.

GIRALDO — ¿Qué dices?

GILA — Llega el oído.

MADALENA — ¿Querrá encargalle su alma?

GILA — Llégate más.

GIRALDO — Ya me llego.

(GILA le muerde en la oreja.)

¿La oreja, ingrata, me arrancas
con los dientes?

GILA — Padre, sí.
Que esto merece quien pasa
por las libertades todas
de los hijos. Si tú usaras
rigor conmigo al principio,
de mi inclinación gallarda

GILA No one need feel any regret
Or bitterness in my death.
I do not see it as a disgrace.
I die content, knowing that
Heaven has willed me to this course.
I am here because of my crimes.
There is no other solution,
Just know, I did it for revenge.
You need not count the robberies,
The many ambushes, assaults;
Focus instead on these two hands
That bear the burden of two thousand lives
For which I now ask pardon.

PASCUALA Madalena, her words claw
At my heart.

MADALENA Yes, Pascuala.

GILA Father! Señor!

GIRALDO What do you want?

GILA I have something I want you to hear.

GIRALDO What is it?

GILA Bring your ear up close.

MADALENA She wants to entrust her soul to him.

GILA Closer.

GIRALDO I'm as close as I can get.

(Gila bites his ear.)

GIRALDO Ungrateful girl! You tear my ear off
With your teeth?!

GILA Yes, father.
Anyone who allows overlooks
The liberties their children take
Deserves a punishment like this.
Had you shown more discipline
When I was young and first inclined

yo no llegara a este estremo.
Escarmienten en tus canas,
y en mí, los que tienen hijos.

GIRALDO Confieso que es justa paga
a mi descuido.

DON JUAN ¡Estraña cosa!
Subid con ella.

(Éntrese con ella agora, y queden PASCUALA y MADALENA.)

MADALENA Pascuala,
¿has visto tal cosa?

PASCUALA El viejo
sangre y lágrimas derrama.

MADALENA Al palo llegan con ella.

PASCUALA Ya la arriman y la atan.

MADALENA Pascuala, los cuadrilleros
se aperciben a tiralla,
que ya el verdugo le pone
el garrote a la garganta.

PASCUALA ¡Perdónete Dios, amén!

MADALENA Esta hue su estrella amarga.
¡Nunca nacieras al mundo!

PASCUALA Mejor hue nacer, pues pasa
desde aquel palo a una vida
que eternamente se acaba.

MADALENA Ya disparan las saetas
los cuadrilleros, Pascuala.

PASCUALA ¡A San Sebastián parece!

(MAESTRE de adentro.)

RODRIGO ¡Aquí es el suplicio! ¡Plaza!

MADALENA ¡Pascuala, estos son los Reyes!

PASCUALA ¡Oh, si primero llegaran!

MADALENA Adrede llegan agora,
porque quieren que su Santa
Hermandad castigue.

	To a daring way of life,
	I would not be here today:
	Let your gray locks be a searing
	Example to anyone daring
	To raise children in this world,
	And let me be an example as well.
GIRALDO	I confess, it's what I deserve for
	My neglect of you.
DON JUAN	Remarkable!
	Bring her on up over here!

(Don Juan exits with Gila. Pascuala and Madalena stay.)

MADALENA	Have you ever seen such a thing?
PASCUALA	The old man's dripping blood and tears.
[MADALENA	They're bringing her to the stake.
PASCUALA	Now they're tying her up.
MADALENA	The troops are loading their arrows.
	They're drawing back their bows.
	The executioner has placed
	The garrote at her throat.
PASCUALA	May God pardon you, amen!
MADALENA	Born under a bitter star:
	Better you had never been born.
PASCUALA	No, better that she was born,
	For she goes straight from that stake
	To a life that eternally
	Ends and ends and ends.
MADALENA	The troops are
	Shooting their arrows, Pascuala.
PASCUALA	She looks like Saint Sebastian.[124]

(The Master speaks, from off stage.)

DON RODRIGO	*[off]* Gaze upon the punishment! Give way!
MADALENA	The King and Queen are entering!
PASCUALA	They came a moment too late!
MADALENA	It's all with express intention,
	So the Brotherhood could inflict
	Their punishment upon her first.

ENTRE DON FERNANDO, y DOÑA ISABEL, y el MAESTRE, y LOS QUE PUDIEREN de acompañamiento, corren el tafetán, y parezca GILA en el palo arriba, llena de saetas y el cabello sobre el rostro, y salgan abajo GIRALDO y DON JUAN.

FERNANDO Ha sido
justo castigo.
MADALENA ¡Bizarra
quedó en el palo también!
ISABEL A mí me enternece el alma.
DON JUAN Este es su padre, señor.
FERNANDO No sé qué merced os haga,
don Juan, por este servicio,
sino es que tengáis la vara
perpetua en Plasencia.
DON JUAN Beso
vuestras generosas plantas.
FERNANDO Y a vos, que luego os entrieguen
el cuerpo para enterralla,
quedando allí una memoria
que de ejemplo sirva a España,
haciéndoos franco también.
GIRALDO Vuestra piedad nos ampara,
que esta fue desdicha mía.
RODRIGO Ya puesto en orden aguarda
de Plasencia el regimiento.
FERNANDO Vamos, señora.
RODRIGO Aquí acaba
la Serrana de la Vera,
que fue prodigio en España.

Laus Deo

FIN DE LA TRAGEDIA DE LA SERRANA DE LA VERA

En Valladolid a 7 de 1613
Luis Vélez de Guevara
Para la señora Jusepa Vaca

Enter Ferdinand and Isabella, and the Master, and everyone available to accompany them. The curtain is drawn, and Gila is seen at the stake, above, full of arrows, her hair covering her face.[125] *Giraldo and Don Juan enter below.*

FERDINAND The punishment is most just.
MADALENA Even on the stake, she is ravishing.
ISABELLA My heart goes tender.
DON JUAN This is the father.
FERDINAND I don't know how to repay this debt,
Don Juan, other than to offer you
In perpetuity, this great symbol,
The mighty staff of Plasencia.
DON JUAN I kiss your generous feet.
FERDINAND And as for you, take her body
And bury it somewhere out here.
May it be a lasting example
To the entire Spanish nation
And keep you honest as well.
GIRALDO Your compassion is my shelter.
She is my lasting disgrace.][126]
DON RODRIGO If everything is in order,
The regiment is waiting.
FERDINAND Let us be going, señora.
DON RODRIGO And so ends Spain's most amazing legend:
La Serrana de la Vera.

Laus Deo[127]

END OF THE TRAGEDY OF LA SERRANA DE LA VERA.

In Valladolid, in the 7th month of 1613.
Luis Vélez de Guevara.
For the señora Juespa Vaca.

NOTES

MP = Manson/Peale edition of *La Serrana de la Vera*
B = Bolaños edition of *La serrana de la Vera*

1 See Introduction for more on Jusepa Vaca, the acclaimed actress for whom Vélez de Guevara wrote the play.

2 The manuscript gives distinct (and incomplete) character lists for each act. I here offer one comprehensive list of speaking characters for the entire play, in order of appearance.

3 See Introduction for more on the Carvajal family. Though the family is historical, the Captain seems to be the playwright's fictional creation.

4 Via their 1469 marriage, Ferdinand and Isabella united their respective kingdoms of Aragon and Castile-Leon, thereby gaining control over the entirety of the Iberian peninsula except for Portugal in the west and the one remaining Moorish kingdom of Granada in the south.

5 Calatrava was a military religious order founded in the 12th century for the purpose of the Crusades. The allegiance of this militia and others like it were vital to Ferdinand and Isabella's gaining control of Iberia amid the peninsular wars of the 15th century. Rodrigo Téllez Girón (1456–1482) was leader of this order at the time of the play's events.

6 This rubric in the manuscript invokes the Holy Family.

7 This rubric in the manuscript acknowledges the playwright's own family: 'Luis' is Vélez. 'Ursola' is his wife, Úrsula. Francisco, Juan, and Antonio are his three sons, the latter of whom was baptized in January 1613, thus helping to date the play. See Peale (2002), 43.

8 I have made the editorial choice of numbering the scenes within each act, as well as giving the likely setting for each scene. None of these scene breaks or locations is present in 17th-century editions of plays. The prevailing logic in staging the plays today is that the modern conception of a scene break – that is, a lapse in time and/or change in location – occurs in a *comedia* whenever all the actors leave the stage.

9 The Captain is *en cuerpo,* meaning he is relatively simply dressed; he has no cape, cloak, or adornments.

10 The play starts in the most common of all *comedia* verse forms: *redondillas*. With the exception of the song accompanying Gila's entrance, Act One continues in *redondillas* until its final 100 lines or so, when the Master of Calatrava delivers his long speech.

11 The Captain is asking Giraldo if he's an *hidalgo*: someone who, though perhaps of modest means, can claim noble lineage.

12 The wordplay in Spanish revolves around *villano*, which can mean peasant or villager as well as rogue or scoundrel.
13 The play is set during the final stage of the Spanish conquest of the remaining Moorish kingdom of Granada – more specifically, as later events show, the battle for Alhama, in 1482. The kingdom finally fell to Ferdinand and Isabella in the fateful year of 1492.
14 La Vera is a region in western Spain, in the north of modern-day Extremadura. It includes the village of Garganta la Olla.
15 Roland: protagonist of the *Chanson de Roland*, French epic poem of the 11th and 12th centuries.
16 In the outdoor *corral* theaters of early modern Spain, the *patio* was the area in front of the stage where most of the audience stood and watched the play. It is roughly comparable to the 'yard' of Shakespearean theater. Her impressive entrance on horseback via the *patio* is highly unusual.
17 Small devotional images or *patenas* were occasionally part of women's attire; folkloric and unusual, they can be glimpsed in representations of early modern nuns. Here they accentuate the striking spectacle of the *serrana*'s entrance.
18 [ ]: Marked for potential omission in the manuscript.
19 'Travelling clothes' (*de camino*) would have been a brightly colored outfit, a feathered hat, and high boots with spurs. See MP 195.
20 This line can be read as a commonplace insult of the time, spoken by a 'pureblood' villager to an urban nobleman. However, as I argue in the Introduction, Gila's anti-Semitic barb is likely pointed and specific, imputing that Carvajals were disreputable *conversos*.
21 Jarandilla, in modern spelling, is a town in La Vera about 25 kilometers by road east of Garganta la Olla. Plasencia lies about 40 kilometers west of Garganta la Olla.
22 Roland: see note 15.
23 The language here evokes an auto-da-fe, another evocation of the Captain's *converso* status.
24 These lines seem out of keeping from Don García, who is urging the Captain to take immediate action. They may be meant ironically.
25 This is one of many places in the play where Vélez paraphrases aphorisms, weaving a popular, folksy quality into the speakers' rhetoric. The First Person's reply is another example.
26 The main open plazas in the center of Spanish towns were generally cordoned off for bullfights for fiestas like this one.
27 *Juego de cañas* was a popular contest of the time. Based in Arab traditions, it involved men on horseback simulating military combat by firing darts made of reeds at each other.
28 Alhama, a town in the kingdom of Granada, was the site of prolonged battled

in 1482 between the Moors and the forces of Ferdinand and Isabella, led by Rodrigo Girón, the Master of Calatrava. Girón died in this battle, though this circumstance is not part of this play.

29 See Character list for more on the Order of Calatrava.

30 Fencing matches were a popular component of fiestas. See MP 199.

31 Andrés's picturesque dress in many ways fulfills the stereotype of young men from small towns.

32 Cuacos: a town about 40 kilometers northeast of Plasencia.

33 The stage business in this section is somewhat unclear. George Peale has communicated to me that he understands Gerónimo to be the barker for the fencing concession, and Perico to be the Master's assistant and designated fighter. In this case, Andrés, with Gerónimo's encouragement, is preparing to fence with Perico.

34 [ ]: Marked for potential omission in the manuscript.

35 [ ]: Marked for potential omission in the manuscript.

36 Isabella's parents were Juan II of Castile and Isabella of Portugal.

37 Juan de Asturias (1478–1497) was Ferdinand and Isabella's only son. The play anachronistically telescopes the siege of Alhama (1482) and Juan's death (1497) into the same historical moment.

38 It is not clear who the Fencing Master is addressing here.

39 [ ]: Marked for potential omission in the manuscript.

40 Andrés mockingly addresses Gila as Don Quixote's object of desire, the servant Aldonza (who he idealizes as the Lady Dulcinea) and Dante's beloved Beatrice from the 13th-century *Divine Comedy*.

41 San Rorro, in the Spanish, is an obscure saint for whom I can find no equivalent in English.

42 Juan or Juanés de la Horta was a famed 16th-century sword-maker, with workshops in Toledo and Valencia.

43 [ ]: Marked for potential omission in the manuscript.

44 [ ]: Marked for potential omission in the manuscript.

45 The *vestuario* – analogous to the Shakespearean tiring house – was accessed through various entrances at the back of the *corral* stage. The implication here is that Gila is going into a curtained 'discovery space' or niche in the center of the *vestuario*, setting up the dramatic tableau to come.

46 The script does not indicate when Don Nuño, the royal servant or advisor, makes his entrance. It is possible he always accompanies Ferdinand and Isabella.

47 The stage direction implies the use of a curtained 'discovery space' that could quickly reveal this tableau. See note 45.

48 See character list for more information.

49 All members of the Calatrava order had an ornate Calatrava cross emblazoned on their shirts.

50 Verse shift to *octavas*.

51 The riches of the Spanish colonial empire in the Caribbean and Latin American were brought back to Spain via two annual fleets that, upon reaching the Mediterranean, sailed up the Guadalquivir River to Seville, Spain's biggest and wealthiest city at the time. Don Rodrigo's reference here is highly anachronistic, since that empire only came into being after Columbus's voyage in 1492.

52 It is not clear whether these refer to specific historic individuals or merely to well-known family names associated with the late 15th-century wars in Granada (both the civil war within the kingdom, and the war against the Christians to the north).

53 Two major towns in the kingdom of Granada.

54 Bucephalus: Alexander the Great's horse.

55 Juana (1479–1555), known as 'Juana la Loca,' became Queen of Spain but exercised little power as she spent the last 40 years of her life incarcerated for mental illness.

56 See notes 6 and 7.

57 See note 45.

58 Act II starts in *redondillas*.

59 Juan Guarín: 9th-century hermit who did penance on the mountain of Montserrat, near Barcelona. See MP 212.

60 [ ]: Marked for potential omission in the manuscript.

61 [ ]: Marked for potential omission in the manuscript.

62 MP, following Rodríguez Cepeda, see the reference (literally, 'ears of Corinth') as being to Corinthian columns, the most sumptuous and adorned of the classical orders. I follow B here, since the grapes metaphor is more consistent with Mingo's rhetoric. Corinthian grapes were unusually small.

63 [ ]: Marked for potential omission in the manuscript.

64 Verse shift to *romance.*

65 [ ]: Marked for potential omission in the manuscript.

66 Verse shift to *endecasílabas*.

67 Giraldo's attitude toward the Captain is changed now from Act One, perhaps due to the Captain's show or force or perhaps because of the Captain's changed attitude.

68 MP notes that this speech may reflect the Carvajals declining position as landowners. To me, it smacks of false humility – part of the Captain's ploy to woe Giraldo and Gila.

69 Wamba: Visigothic ruler of 7th-century Spain.

70 Prester John is a legendary Christian ruler who figured prominently in the imagination of the European Renaissance. He was associated with Asian or African exotic lands at the fringes of Christianity.

71 Gila and its male counterpart Gil were names stereotypically associated with rural people in *comedias* – most famously, in Tirso de Molina's *Don Gil de las calzas verdes*.

72 The Captain evokes powerful, sometimes violent women rulers from the past: Semiramis, legendary queen of ancient Assyria; Evadne, tragic figure of ancient Argos, known as a fierce woman warrior; and the Greek goddess of wisdom and warfare, Athena.

73 The approval that Don García was seeking in Salamanca is obscure, and not important to the action of the play.

74 Verse shift to *romance.* The longest of a number of long speeches in the play, no part of it is set aside in the manuscript for cutting, suggesting that these bravura set pieces, delivered by commanding actors, were a performative highlight in the *corrales*.

75 De la Parra was a famed physician who attended on Ferdinand and Isabella. Galen was a celebrated Greek physician of the Roman era, and Asclepius a hero/god of medicine.

76 See note 55.

77 He actually had four. See B 200.

78 Arcady and Ephesus denote ancient Greece and Troy, respectively.

79 I have taken some liberties in rendering this list of architectural features to capture the hyperbolic, highly technical quality of the rhetoric.

80 These special guards, at the time of the play's writing, kept constant vigil over the King and Queen, among other important duties. See MP 226.

81 This is another anachronism, as she would not assume power until 1500, three years after her brother's death.

82 Verse shift to *endecasílabas*.

83 His twin brother, Don Alonso Téllez Girón.

84 Archidona and Morón de la Frontera are towns in southern Spain, to the west of Granada.

85 See note 72.

86 This may be a reference to young King Boabdil, Muhammed II, who was aligned with Ferdinand and Isabella during the siege of Málaga in 1487.

87 The references here are all to historical personages, named in the chronicles of the Reconquest of Granada.

88 Verse shift to *redondillas*.

89 The Estúñigas or Zúñigas were a branch of the illustrious Béjar family.

90 Verse shift to *romance*.

91 Minor characters that appear in Canto X of Ariosto's early 16th-century epic *Orlando Furioso*, a tremendously popular work in Golden Age Spain. Parallel to the circumstances here, Bireno abandons his lover Olimpia while she is

sleeping – indeed, stranding her on an island as he sails away with his fleet. I have glossed these circumstances into the translation.

92 See notes 6 and 7.

93 The script does not indicate when the Traveler enters. I have placed his entrance at the last possible moment, allowing for Gila to be on stage while his song, off stage, describes her.

94 The dialogue in most of this act implies a multi-level use of space, with Gila's cabin being located on an upper level, as distinct from the lower level through which travelers enter the sierra. The *corrales* had balconies to accommodate this staging, as well as the possibility of ramps or stairways to allow for ascents/descents between levels.

95 [ ]: Marked for potential omission in the manuscript.

96 Quiteria was patron saint of blindness and rabies, among other ailments.

97 The dialogue implies some physical comedy where Gila has tried to ride Mingo. It ends at this stage direction, which I have slightly relocated accordingly.

98 Dismas, known as the Penitent Thief, was one of the men crucified alongside Christ.

99 [ ]: Marked for potential omission in the manuscript.

100 The Brotherhood, or Hermandad, was a powerful rural police force in Castile. As the action of the play will reveal, it enjoyed certain prerogatives that could not readily be challenged by the monarchs. See B 244.

101 It is not established elsewhere in the play that Mingo is part of Gila's household, whether as a servant or (like Madalena) a cousin.

102 The manuscript does not mark the entrance of Gila. I have placed her entrance at the most logical place.

103 [ ]: Marked for potential omission in the manuscript.

104 Reference to an ancestral Girón, Don Rodrigo González de Cisneros, who legendarily lent King Alfonso VI a horse when the Moors had killed his in a 14th-century battle. See MP 240.

105 A collarless cape derived from those worn in Germany.

106 Verse shift to *endecasílabas*.

107 Monks and students were popularly represented as living in poverty.

108 [ ]: Marked for potential omission in the manuscript. Andrés's line invokes Apollo's chariot.

109 The villagers are taking part in a *romería*, a Spanish rural tradition that involves pastoral religious processions and celebrations.

110 What the villagers sing is citational of one of the versions of the traditional ballad that inspired this play. See Introduction.

111 Verse shift to *redondillas*.

112 [ ]: Marked for potential omission in the manuscript.
113 [ ]: Marked for potential omission in the manuscript.
114 Verse shift to *décimas*.
115 [ ]: Marked for potential omission in the manuscript.
116 This piece of exposition clarifies that Don Lucas has been to Granada and back during the interim between Acts Two and Three (as has presumably Don Rodrigo).
117 [ ]: Marked for potential omission in the manuscript.
118 [ ]: Marked for potential omission in the manuscript.
119 The geographical location is not specified, Ferdinand and Isabella having no fixed court or capital. The location may be presumed to be Salamanca, since this is where we have seen them before, and Salamanca would give them easy access to Plasencia, where the play ends.
120 Verse shift to *tercetos*.
121 These brotherhoods were far from new, although the one in Castile received new authority from Isabella in 1476. B, 293, notes that this branch was effectively an arm of the Spanish Inquisition, which had also been granted new authority in parts of Castile, c. 1480–1481.
122 [ ]: This entire short scene is marked for potential omission in the manuscript.
123 Verse shift to *romance.*
124 Early Christian saint persecuted by the Romans, commonly depicted as tied to a tree or stake and pierced by multiple arrows.
125 Once again, this moment requires a so-called 'discovery space.' The sudden running of the curtain could reveal tableaux like this one. Here, the discovery space seems to be in the balcony.
126 [ ]: Marked for potential omission in the manuscript.
127 Latin: 'praise God.'